S0-BCN-964

SPIRITUALITY

Toward a 21st Century Lutheran Understanding

Kirsi Stjerna
Brooks Schramm
Editors

Lutheran University Press
Minneapolis, Minnesota

SPIRITUALITY
Toward a 21st Century Lutheran Understanding
Kirsi Stjerna and Brooks Schramm, Editors

Copyright © 2004 Lutheran University Press. All rights reserved. Except for brief quotations in critical articles or reviews, no part of this book may be reproduced in any manner without prior permission of the publisher.

Library of Congress Cataloging-in Publication Data

Spirituality : toward a 21st century Lutheran understanding / Kirsi Stjerna, Brooks Schramm, editors
     p.cm.
   Includes bibliographic references
   ISBN 1-932688-04-8 (alk. paper)
     1. Spirituality—Lutheran Church. 2. Lutheran Church—Doctrines. I. Stjerna, Kirsi Irmeli, 1963- II. Schramm, Brooks, 1957-

BX 8065.3.S68 2004
248".088'2841—dc22

2004052969

Lutheran University Press, PO Box 390759, Minneapolis, MN 55439
Manufactured in the United States of America

Table of Contents

Introduction

Spirituality is an "in" word today, with many definitions and trends associated with it. One can hardly turn on the TV or open a magazine without encountering the word. Or, try checking out the offerings on the worldwide web! It is popular to "be spiritual" and "talk spiritual"—even without having a clear idea of what that might actually mean. The way the word is commonly used today makes one wonder: what makes "spirituality" anything different from being alive and breathing as a spirited, living creature?

In many vocabularies the word "spirituality" refers in one way or another to a search or a yearning for wholeness and meaning, finding and connecting with "ultimate values," having a sense of purpose in life, living with a belief system that supports one in all aspects of life. The common goal in various spiritualities appears to be a life with a meaning and an overall satisfaction and assurance that "all is well," as Julian of Norwich describes a spiritually attuned approach to life.

In contemporary use, the words "wholeness," "holistic life and health," and "spirituality" seem to be interchangeable. They are used as ways of expressing the human search for a meaningful life. Though it would have been impossible for our medieval foremothers and fathers to imagine spirituality without God, today, however, it is possible, as new kinds of spiritualities around central values other than God are emerging and offering people sustaining meanings in life.

In Christian tradition spirituality used to be associated, in a narrow sense, with specific people with a specific call in their search for union with God and for a privileged knowledge and experience of God. In today's conversations, the trend is to consider spirituality not as the privilege of the few but as something that belongs to all. In today's world, spirituality does not need to be defined by using traditional religious terminology and God-talk. The rules for defining "spiritual needs" and talking about "spiritual living" have changed so dramatically that it has become difficult to know what exactly spirituality is.

In contemporary Protestant contexts, there is considerable ambiguity around the word spirituality, and for some the whole concept is readily dismissed as a mere "trendy" phase that will soon pass away. As "trendy" as the word is in the broader culture, our contention is that the concept of spirituality is about something vital to Christianity. The very popularity of the word can serve as an impetus for Christian theologians, believers and practitioners to recover and explicate something that is fundamental to the faith.

Alistair McGrath in his book, *Christian Spirituality*, describes spirituality as something that "concerns the quest for a fulfilled and authentic religious life, involving the bringing together of the ideas distinctive of that religion and the whole experience of living on the basis of and within the scope of that religion." Further, "[s]pirituality is the outworking in real life of a person's religious faith—what a person does with what they believe. It is not just about ideas, although the basic ideas of the Christian faith are important to Christian spirituality. It is about the way in which the Christian life is conceived and lived out." Also, "Christian spirituality is reflection on the whole Christian enterprise of achieving and sustaining a relationship with God, which includes both public worship and private devotion, and the result of these in actual Christian life" (McGrath 1999, 2). This definition serves as a good starting point and helps to show how spirituality has to do with basic things.

Richard McBrien in his book, *Lives of the Saints from Mary and St. Francis of Assisi to John XXIII and Mother Teresa*, says, "[t]o be 'spiritual' means to know and to live according to the knowledge that there is more to life than meets the eye. The 'more than' is the sacred, the holy, the transcendent, the supernatural, the divine-Christian spirituality, therefore, has to do with a way of being Christian, that is, of being a disciple of

Christ. Christian spirituality is rooted in the life of the triune God, centered on Jesus Christ, animated by the Holy Spirit, lived out within the Church and the wider world, and oriented always to the coming of God's Reign in all its fullness at the end of human history" (McBrien 2001, 18).

In its different expressions, Christian spirituality is visionary, sacramental, relational and transformational. In tune with this view, Christian spirituality can be characterized as spirituality centered around the notion of a triune God who, as a majority of Christians believe, became incarnate and continues to sustain and create life and sanctify through the Spirit. Christian spirituality arises from the premise of who Christians think God is and how God acts in creation.

Though there is obvious diversity within Christian types of spiritualities, there are basic tenets which are held in common: belief in God as the creator and source of life, belief in God's real presence, search for and celebration of the ways through which God is in relation with creation, finding ways to celebrate that relationship on a personal as well as a communal level, and an intention or desire to be guided by the purpose deriving from that relationship.

Spirituality is inherently linked with theology. Spirituality without theology is without substantive content, meaning, and direction. On the other hand, one could also say that spirituality makes theology concrete. Episcopalian theologian Mark McIntosh in his *Mysteries of Faith* has articulated a view on "living theologically," and his words can be taken to describe what spirituality and living spiritually can be about when spirituality is understood as inherently linked with theology. According to McIntosh, "[t]heology is about seeing the meaning of things in the context of life with God. . . .Theology is about seeking out and listening to that meaning, hearing it not just as any kind of meaning but as God's meaning" (McIntosh 2000, 2).

The thoughts described above are not alien to Lutheran theology and practice, although the language of spirituality may seem novel to many contemporary Lutherans who associate spirituality with a specific type ("Catholic," "New Age," "mystical," etc.) of religiosity, religious experience, or discipline. In a way, Lutheran tradition is in the process of reclaiming and embracing the word that has been implicitly a part of Lutheran believing and living. Drawing on Luther's unique interpretation of what is holy, what vocation is, and where and how God is present, Lutherans have historically lived a theologically rooted, unpretentious spirituality.

Lutherans have believed in God's real presence in the world, in the power of God to work in human lives through Word and sacrament. Lutherans have taught the catechism to their children as a form of discipline and for the formation of beliefs, and have taken the Scripture as the basis of revelation about God. Around these beliefs, Lutherans have formed communal ways of worship and related their shared faith to the "world" through mission and humanitarian work. Spirituality, thus, has been taught and lived among Lutherans in various ways, without "thinking" of it as something separate from what being Lutheran or Christian means but as something that is implicitly and concretely lived out in Christian communities of faith.

The writers of this book will examine the concept of "spiri-tuality" in and in relation to different disciplines and will show how inclusive, broad, and complex the term spirituality can be. While demonstrating the diversity and complexity of the con-cept, the writers start with a common understanding of what Lutheran spirituality rests on: the central Lutheran emphasis on God's promise to work in the world through the Word and the sacraments, and the Lutheran teaching of justification by grace through faith alone. At the core of Lutheran spirituality there is a particular pneumatology which speaks of the omnipresence and effective sustaining work of the Spirit in creation, in all its dimensions. This allows for a broad, realistic and humble under-standing of the sacred, in light of a fundamental respect for the immanence and mystery of the Divine.

The starting point for all of the articles in this book is an appreciation of the broadness of the term spirituality, and the premise is that spirituality is about living a life with God and that there is more than one way to "do" and speak about that. The articles will examine spirituality in its historic and contemporary expressions in Christian and especially Lutheran contexts, in various areas of teaching—biblical study, theology, history, ethics, worship, Christian education, counseling, stewardship, practical theology, ministry—as well as in worship life and administration, all areas dealing with but not limited to theological education.

As theological education is a crucial part of the training of Lutheran leaders who are called to serve in roles of spiritual leadership in their varied positions, discussion here is intended to benefit seminary students and teachers. Furthermore, the discussion is also applicable to "inquirers" and, indeed, for all "practioners" of the faith, both clergy and laity, who want to embrace spirituality in meaningful ways in their specific context.

The articles will demonstrate the inclusivity as well as the specificity of the word spirituality and also the continuity with the main building blocks and elements in any spirituality— Christian, Lutheran or "other" kinds. The primary purpose is not to present a definite, closed "Lutheran definition" of "Lutheran spirituality" but rather to demonstrate where the areas of unity and continuity are and where the unemployed possibilities are for both educational purposes and for fostering the spiritualities of people in different stations in life.

This book is a tribute to the late Professor Bengt Hoffman, who during his tenure in the Lutheran Theological Seminary at Gettysburg wrote about the importance of the spiritual dimension in Luther's theology, beginning with his controversial book *Luther and the Mystics* (1976), recently republished in a revised version as *Theology of the Heart* (1998). A grant from the Hoffman foundation is sponsoring this project, with the personal support of Mrs. Pearl Hoffman. Another grant that makes this book possible comes from the Pitcairn-Crabbe foundation, granted to the seminary in 1998 for envisioning and implementing spiritual formation in theological education.

As a response to the need for articulated views and sources on spirituality in today's theological education and in ministry, the faculty and selected staff of the seminary offer, through their perspectives and expertise, material and insights for thinking about and teaching the subject. The essays in this book present issues and views rising from specific disciplines. Some demonstrate how spirituality is inherent in different aspects of theological education and disciplines that deal with religion and religiosity (e.g., Lutheran history as history of spirituality; religiosity and piety of immigrants in North America; spiritual formation, congregational life and internship; worship traditions and spirituality). Some articles discuss ways to bring the subject of spirituality to the classroom in a particular discipline or ways to see a specific field as soil for the study of spirituality and spiritual formation (e.g., Christian education and spirituality; pastoral counseling and spiritual formation). Some articles present specific contributions from a special field to further understanding of the concept, study and teaching of spirituality (e.g., biblical study, historical study of different forms of spirituality and spiritual teachers). Some articles are more theoretical, some more practical; in other words, some authors focus on theoretical issues of the study of or the teaching of spirituality, and some relate their conclusions more clearly to application and possibilities there, and this especially in the context of theological education. While the audience is in no way imagined to be limited to people involved currently in theological education, it is our hope that readers will benefit from the expertise of scholars in theological education, scholars who are actively involved in the life of the church and different ministries there through their teaching vocation.

In their own ways, the authors demonstrate or model how different theologies and practices of spirituality are dealt with and paid attention to in theological education and in ministry. In this way the authors help to identify some of the central issues, sources, possibilities and perspectives regarding spirituality, ministry and theological education, and offer some suggestions on how spirituality can be seen as inherent and central in all Christian thinking, speaking, and living.

Three general themes regarding Christian spirituality will be seen as held in common by our Lutheran writers. First, Christian spirituality is incarnational. Second, meaningful spirituality becomes manifest in outward orientation rather than merely being something for the benefit of the practicing individual. Third, the word spirituality is not regarded as irreducible.

This book is not a devotional book or a traditional academic book on the study of spirituality, or a book on the history of spirituality. It does not treat spirituality as a separate discipline but as part of the whole. The perspectives presented are those of a diverse group of educators, not necessarily heavily invested in a specialized study of spirituality per se. Even if all the authors represent a Lutheran institution, the book has an ecumenical interest in that articles arising out of specific academic disciplines can speak to individuals regardless of their denominational affiliation.

Interdisciplinary views on the subject will show how spirituality does not need to be a separate part of the curriculum in theological education any more than it needs to be a specialized form of ministry or a compartmentalized place of faith life in general, but can and needs to be an inherent part of the whole of Christian living and being.

Kirsi Stjerna

References

Hoffman, Bengt R. 1998. *Theology of the Heart: The Role of Mysticism in the Theology of Martin Luther.* Edited by Pearl Willemssen Hoffman. Minneapolis: Kirkhouse Press.

Hoffman, Bengt R. 1976. *Luther and the Mystics: A Re-Examination of Luther's Spiritual Experience and His Relationship to the Mystics.* Minneapolis: Augsburg Publishing House.

Jones, Cheslyn, Geoffrey Wainwright, and Edward Yarnold, S.J., eds. 1986. *The Study of Spirituality.* New York: Oxford University Press.

McBrien, Richard. 2001. *Lives of the Saints from Mary and St. Francis of Assisi to John XXIII and Mother Teresa.* SanFrancisco: Harper Collins.

McGrath, Alistair. 1999. *Christian Spirituality: An Introduction.* Oxford: Blackwell Publishers.

McIntosh, Mark. 2000. *Mysteries of Faith.* Cambridge, Mass: Cowley Publications.

Mursell, Gordon, ed. 2001. *The Story of Christian Spirituality, Two Thousands Years, From East to West.* Minneapolis: Fortress Press.

Other sources for overviews on Christian spirituality

Dupré, Louis and Don E. Saliers, eds. 1991. *Christian Spirituality: Post-Reformation and Modern.* World Spirituality: An Encyclopedic History of the Religious Quest, vol. 18. New York: Crossroad.

Healey, Charles J. 1999. *Christian Spirituality: An Introduction to the Heritage.* New York: Alba House.

McGinn, Bernard and John Meyendorff, eds. 1985. *Christian Spirituality: Origins to the Twelfth Century.* World Spirituality: An Encyclopedic History of the Religious Quest, vol. 16. New York: Crossroad.

Raitt, Jill, ed. 1987. *Christian Spirituality: High Middle Ages and Reformation.* World Spirituality: An Encyclopedic History of the Religious Quest, vol. 17. New York: Crossroad.

Spirituality, Spiritual Formation, and Preparation for Pastoral Ministry

J. Paul Balas

Spirituality and spiritual formation have not been common words in historical Lutheran parlance, nor have the concepts and understandings underlying them been seen popularly as foundational for the faith. Instead, words such as grace, law, gospel, justification, sin, and forgiveness have served to describe the fundamentals of the Lutheran understanding of life lived before God (*coram deo*). But things have begun to change (attested to by the writings in this volume), perhaps out of a need to keep up with a cultural/religious trend, a need to refocus and regroup in order to protect market share in a time of mainline religious downsizing and stocktaking, or a need to re-mine, revalue, and restate the basics of the tradition. Time may tell. In any case, one of the issues precipitated by this change has been the issue of the role, function, and shape of spirituality and spiritual formation in the formal preparation of those persons in the seminaries of the church who are moving toward ministerial vocations.

After many years of assumptive silence, the church as institution has begun both to speak and to act with regard to this issue. The Evangelical Lutheran Church in America's Division for Ministry now prescribes "spiritual formation" as one of its required "Academic and Practical Criteria for Ordination." "Personal spiritual formation" is also listed as a criterion to be met as a requirement for "Consecrated Diaconal Ministry" in the church. One of The Lutheran Theological Seminary at Gettysburg's "Eight Directions for the Decade" is to "Foster Spiritual Development." It reads: "The seminary's formation of enrolled students, as well as those involved in lifelong learning offerings, will seek to instill and ingrain a deep sense of spirituality grounded in the Word of God and flowing from the means of grace." Many synodical candidacy committees of the Evangelical Lutheran Church in America see "spiritual direction" as a foundational tool for "spiritual formation" and require it of their candidates. The curriculum of Gettysburg Seminary now has courses in or related to spirituality, whereas in the past of memory, there were none.

There is also some hesitation, even suspicion, about the fitness of Lutherans even to entertain discussion about spirituality and spiritual formation. Paul S. Lundborg's Doctor of Ministry dissertation/project entitled, "Spiritual Formation: An Ancient Practice for Lutheran Parish Life Today," contains an interesting and informative discussion about this. In it Lundborg says the following:

> Many Lutheran people today, upon first hearing about spirituality, might quickly consign this concept to the realm of the subjective, the mystical, and consequently the suspect. Unthinking, they might contrast heady, theologically sound Lutheranism with spirituality.... Although Luther had a spiritual father, Johannes Staupitz, and Luther wrote letters of spiritual counsel to other believers, he so thoroughly rejected anything that reminded him of the monastery that it is highly unlikely he would have called for spiritual direction among his followers.... My experience has been that no training in spiritual practices and methods exists in Lutheran churches. . . . Many Lutheran clergy are unwilling and unable to teach . . . classes involving methods because in their seminary training they have not been exposed to classes on the spiritual life (Lundborg 1991, 17, 34, 41).

In addition, I find that many in the Lutheran faith community who are doing spiritual formation, teaching about spirituality, and either giving or receiving spiritual direction are not turning to their tradition for the basis of their work. This was brought home to me by a Lutheran pastor colleague, a degreed specialist in spirituality and spiritual direction, who, in my hearing, said the following to a gathering of newly ordained Lutheran pastors during a three-day "first call theological education" event: "Don't trust your people, the church, to help you with your pastoral identity. Go straight to God. Get a spiritual director—not a Lutheran! They don't know anything about this. Go to the sisters. A spiritual director knows how to connect with God."

This essay is an attempt to make some suggestions about how the issue of spirituality and spiritual formation might be addressed in one seminary of the ELCA. It does not intend to be definitive, directive, dogmatic, or parochial. The intent is primarily to enter as one voice into the broader conversation about the understanding, shape, function, and place of spirituality and spiritual formation in theological education. As a part of that conversation, I hope to present some possibilities about how one might approach the issue, how one might proceed, and where and how one might look for basic form and content. On the other hand, it is hoped that the ideas and possibilities put forth here might be relevant beyond the realm of theological education, relevant especially to the pastors and parishioners gathered to hear the preaching of the Word and to receive the sacraments who, after all, constitute the church. Last, but certainly not least, this writing is intended to be an exercise in pastoral theology. As such, it is an attempt to reclaim as central an historic but neglected task of the discipline: that of theologically and practically shaping both the office of the ministry and the persons called to serve in that office.

The essay begins with an explication of two distinct dimensions of spirituality as these have historically presented themselves in the church catholic and particularly in Lutheranism. A critical review of contemporary attempts at renewal and recovery of the Lutheran tradition, especially the efforts of one seminary, follows. The chapter closes with a plea for the inclusion of the two aforementioned distinctive dimensions of spirituality in contemporary Lutheran seminary education, and for the addition of a third, integrative element.

Spirituality's Two Dimensions

In a chapter entitled, "The Meaning of Mysticism from Meister Eckhart to Martin Luther," Luther scholar Heiko Oberman describes the spiritual tradition of the Western Church in this way:

> Within the concept of faith there are two 'dimensions:' the first is the belief that the articles of faith are true. Faith in this sense is the acknowledgement of the 'great deeds' in God's creation, incarnation, passion, resurrection, and glorification. This faith requires us to defer to the authority of Scripture or the Church. In Latin, this dimension of acknowledgement is designated by the term *fides quae creditur*: that is, the articles of faith that are believed and accepted. . . .
>
> The second dimension is termed in Latin *fides qua creditur* (faith by which one believes): faith as a position or attitude vis-à-vis God, a relationship with God
>
> Faith . . . associated with *fides qua creditur*, one's living association with God, can never be separated from *fides quae creditur*, the articles of faith. A living association with God can be imagined only within a complementary or even a tense relationship to faith in revealed truth as the necessary foundation of *fides qua creditur*. . . . The experience of faith cannot circumvent the Confession of Faith (Oberman 1994, 77).

Oberman's statement points to a fundamental aspect of spirituality and spiritual formation as it has manifested itself historically in Western Christianity, especially so in the Lutheran tradition. The faith by which one believes—*fides qua creditur*, the process of having faith, doing faith, "faithing," relating to God, expressing one's relationship to God, in the popular use of the word, "spirituality"—never exists apart from the faith that one believes—*fides quae creditur*, the articles of faith that one accepts, the confession of faith that one makes, the content of faith.

Interestingly, this historical/theological observation is affirmed psychologically and developmentally by George Vaillant, a widely respected psychiatrist, researcher, and medical school professor. In his review and explication of "The Harvard

Study of Adult Development," a 60 year plus longitudinal research project following the lives of three disparate cohorts of about 750 individuals, which he now directs, Vaillant says the following about *fides qua creditur* and *fides quae creditur*:

> Religion involves creeds and catechisms. Spirituality involves feelings and experiences that transcend mere words. Religion is imitative and comes from without; religion is "so I've been taught." Spirituality comes from within; spirituality comes from "my strength, hope, and experience." Religion is "left-brain"—it is rooted in words, sacred texts, and culture. Spirituality is "right-brain;" it transcends the boundaries of body, language, reason, and culture. However, just as both sides of the brain are inseparable, just so for most people religion and spirituality are inseparable. . . .Both . . . reflect faith (Vaillant 2002, 260).

This truth about the inseparability of faith's two dimensions is a major factor in differentiating Christian spirituality from the many, varied, and ubiquitous "spiritualities" that permeate American culture today. Bill Broadway, a writer for *The Washington Post* describes the situation from the perspective of the American market place:

> Talk of soul and spirituality is flowing freely in the workplace these days. . . . Alternately called spiritual economics, soul in the workplace, and values driven leadership, this is a quasi-religious movement, one without a god or theological foundation, but filled with moral attitudes and guidelines common to all religions. . . .The size of the trend is hard to quantify, but there are signs of growing interest in finding common ground between business and religion (Broadway 2001, A1, A6).

Spirituality for Christians, however, is different and includes a defined theological foundation, a belief in a particular god, and a particular trust in a god who is described and understood in a distinctive and particular way.

Spirituality and Lutherans

Historically, a deep rooting in a theological foundation, in a *fides quae creditur*, has been a central and defining aspect of lived faith for Lutherans. I would go so far as to say that it is one of the distinctive strengths of the Lutheran spiritual tradition.

Luther himself expressed this quite forcefully in his explanation of the first commandment in his "Large Catechism." He includes both the activity of faith and the content or object of faith in his discussion, pointing insightfully to their determinative interaction. False faith trusts in a false god; true faith trusts in the true God. Faith in the true God is the central issue.

> A "god" is the term for that to which we are to look for all good and in which we find refuge in time of need. Therefore to have a God is nothing else than to trust and believe in one with your whole heart. As I have often said, it is the trust and faith of the heart alone that make both God and an idol. If your faith and trust are right, then your God is the true one. Conversely, where your trust is false and wrong, then you do not have the true God. For these two belong together, faith and God. Anything on which your heart relies and depends, I say, that is really your God. The intention of this commandment, therefore, is to require true faith and confidence of the heart, which fly straight to the one true God and cling to him alone (Luther 1529, 386).

For Luther, the "true" practice of faith is mutually and inextricably related to the "true" object of faith. One cannot exist apart from the other. "Spirituality," understood by Luther as life lived before God, must include and involve both.

Bradley Hanson, a Lutheran theologian with a comprehensive grasp of and a deep interest in Lutheran faith and spirituality, describes it in this way: "The Lutheran faith is . . . thoroughly informed by a coherent theological vision. . . . What counts most is the theological vision that informs the spirituality (Hanson 2000, x)."

Hanson also sets forth (accurately, I judge) what he describes as seven "characteristics of Lutheran spirituality," stating that, "[w]hile other Christian spiritual traditions may share in one or several of these characteristics, only Lutheran spirituality manifests all seven of them." True to his understanding of the theological basis of Lutheran spirituality, each of Hanson's characteristics summarizes an essential belief of the Lutheran tradition. The characteristics include:

Conviction that alienation from God is the deep and persistent root of our problems as individuals and communities.

Trust that God's merciful grace undergirds all of life.

Reliance on the word of God in Scripture, proclamation, and music as the primary source of spiritual nurture and guidance.

Confidence that God's grace is present in the sacraments of baptism and the Lord's supper and may also work through other rites, gestures, and physical objects.

Participation in the communal life of the church with responsibility for the nurture of one another.

Deep loyalty to core church traditions as expressed in the classic creeds and Lutheran confessions and both respect and freedom toward secondary traditions.

Conviction that God's twofold rule summons all people to seek justice and calls Christians to faithful service in their daily relationships in life (Hanson 2000, 18).

Lutheran ethicist, Robert Benne, refers to this aspect of Lutheran identity (*fides quae creditur*) as its "core vision." He states: "The church must attend to its core vision by proclaiming it and attempting to be faithful to it through its practice. . . .The core vision should be held with clarity and confidence by the church" (Benne 1998, 20).

Luther scholar and historian Eric Gritsch elaborates on how the Lutheran tradition's deep valuing of its theological foundations goes back to Luther himself, and to Luther's understanding of theological clarity as a sign of faithfulness.

Luther believed in the orthodoxy of conflict, therapeutic conflict, as it were, whereby true believers remain faithful. They must do battle with the diabolical forces (from the Greek *diaballein*, 'to deceive') in the church and the world. If they don't, they become confused and, once confused, will fall into the hands of Satan. According to Luther, Satan is only interested in places where the gospel is present, which is why the church must endure suffering and conflict (Gritsch 1983).

Here Gritsch points out that for Luther, and for Lutherans, "the gospel," as the content dimension of faith, forms the foundation for the process dimension of faith, and as such, is essential to spiritual formation and practice. For Luther and for Lutherans, explicit clarity about what and in whom one believes (one's theology) is a *sine qua non* for faithfulness in the expression and living out of that belief (spiritual practice). The church and its leaders must be willing to fight and to suffer for such clarity, says Gritsch. Why? Because a lack of clarity about the content of faith leads to theological confusion, and theological confusion leads to spiritual unfaithfulness (trusting in a false God or a false understanding of God), a sure sign that Satan—the evil one, according to Jewish and Christian tradition—is in control.

What then of the practice of faith, *fides qua creditur*, the faith by which one believes, the process of faith? Where and how does that dimension of faith fit within the Lutheran spiritual tradition? It is essential, integral, and complementary to the other spiritual dimension of faith, *fides quae creditur*. Luther was deeply committed to the spiritual practices of faith. At the same time he was flexible about how these might be carried out in both individual and communal life.

With regard to prayer he was both dedicated and disciplined, praying for hours each morning and adding more on those mornings that preceded especially busy or challenging days of work. As to how individual Christians might go about this, he was suggestive, having no need to impose his personal practices upon others. In "A Simple Way to Pray," a small manual written for his barber, Peter Beskendorf, who was also one of his oldest and dearest friends, Luther says the following about prayer:

> I will tell you as best I can what I do personally when I pray. May the Lord grant to you and to everybody to do it better than I. . . . It is a good thing to let prayer be the first business of the morning and the last at night. . . .We must be careful not to break the habit of true prayer. . . .To this day I suckle at the Lord's prayer like a child, and as an old man eat and drink from it and never get my fill (Luther 1535, 193, 194, 200).

The reading of scripture as an individual spiritual exercise was also of central importance to Luther. This, as with other spiritual practices, he adapted to and integrated with his emphasis on the gospel, and, in this specific case, to his belief that the devil was always present when one was engaging God's word, tempting him/her to do otherwise. His transformation of the medieval church's formula for spiritual reading from *lectio, oratio, meditatio, contemplatio* (reading, prayer, meditation, contemplation) to *oratio, meditatio, tentatio* (prayer, meditation, struggle) is indicative of this. For Luther, it is participation in this kind of struggle that would form one into a real theologian. "For as soon as God's Word takes root and grows in you the devil will harry you, and will make a real doctor of you, and by his assaults will teach you to seek and love God's Word" (Luther 1539, 67).

Unlike the more radical reformers, Luther did not abandon the Western Church's liturgical/musical and aesthetic/artistic forms of communal faith expression as means for spiritual nurture. Instead, he appreciatively adapted them both to his cultural context and to his theological passion for the gospel, which he understood in the way interpreted and explicated by St. Paul in the New Testament as "justification by grace through faith." In his "Smalcald Articles," he describes these forms as ways in which the gospel gives help against sin, listing the spoken word, baptism, the Sacrament of the Altar, the power of the keys, and the mutual conversation and consolation of brothers and sisters as definitive examples or means (Luther, 1537, 319).

From the viewpoint of pastoral theology, it is significant that confession and absolution (described by Luther in the "Smalcald Articles" as the power of the keys and the mutual conversation and consolation of the brothers and sisters) became the primary form of individual spiritual counsel and guidance in the faith community that gathered around Luther and his spiritual teachings and practices (McNeill 1965, 163 ff.). This was almost lost, however, in the American experience, when private confession's association with Roman Catholicism led to its decline among Lutherans (Wentz 1964, 136).

In many twentieth century Lutheran Churches in the United States, as was the case in much of mainline American Protestantism also, the increase in the popularity of psychology and psychotherapy as ways of dealing with the strains and stresses of life, including religious life, had a major additional effect. Here the practice of spiritual counsel was gradually replaced by an emphasis on pastoral counseling/psychotherapy, which became a predominant form of pastoral care in Lutheran and especially Protestant mainline churches during the second half of the twentieth century (Hollifield 1983; Gerkin 1997, 53ff). Sociologist Robert Wuthnow summarizes the phenomenon as "'the therapeutic turn' in American religion. God doesn't tell you what to do, just makes you feel better about what you were going to do anyway. The therapeutic turn means that religion, like therapy, serves mainly to make us feel good" (Wuthnow 2003, 11).

Recent discussions at the meetings and in the journals of pastoral theological societies and associations are an indication that the situation with regard to this issue may be changing. Rodney J. Hunter's words, delivered to an annual meeting of the Society for Pastoral Theology, seem to illustrate this.

> The need of the hour is to shift the basic understanding of pastoral care and counseling from a primarily therapeutic orientation to one that is principally ecclesial. . . . The creation of strong, durable religious communities and individuals within these communities should be two of the basic aims of practical theology in general and pastoral theology in particular. Healing, the principal norm and guiding metaphor of twentieth century pastoral care and counseling, must continue to be relativised and reconceived as an important but finally subordinate component of committed participation in Christian *ecclesia*. . . . The great problem for many people otherwise inclined toward Christian faith seems to be institutional affiliation: they regard spirituality as a private affair and resist joining churches and committing themselves to demanding programs and belief systems (except, perhaps to provide moral education for their children). . . . From a theological perspective, in the mainstream of Christian tradition, faith is intimately connected with committed membership in sacred community: to believe is to belong, to be a member of the Body of Christ as branches participate in the vine (Hunter 1998, 16, 17).

Recovery and Renewal of the Tradition

There are now very concrete signs of a renewed appreciation for and recovery of the Lutheran spiritual tradition within the Evangelical Lutheran Church in America. Indications of this in the bureaucratic and institutional life of the church were mentioned above. An elementary computer search will reveal that there has also been a substantial surge in the publication of both academic and more popular books and articles dealing with the subject. Conferences, colloquies, institutes, and forums on the topic of spirituality abound. The "new" Finnish interpretations of this aspect of Luther's theology (Braaten and Jenson 1998), and a renewal of interest in the work of Bengt R. Hoffman, in whose honor and memory this volume is dedicated (Hoffman 2003), have played and continue to play their part in all of this.

A major step toward this renewal among the seminaries of the ELCA was taken when "Spirituality and Spiritual Formation: A Position Paper of the Faculty of Lutheran Theological Southern Seminary," in Columbia, South Carolina, was adopted by a unanimous vote by said faculty on October 9, 1998, "as a guide and reference point for discussion and action within the Seminary community, and as a responsible contribution to ongoing discussion within the wider church" (Faculty of Lutheran Theological Southern Seminary 1998). This is a thoughtful, balanced, comprehensive, well written, sensitive, thoroughly researched and documented, and creative piece of writing that should serve its purpose well.

Bradley Hanson writes the following about the paper: "I'm happy to say that I agree almost entirely with what is stated there; my differences are mostly in emphasis or certain uses of terminology" (Hansen 2000, x). This writer would, for the most part, agree with Hanson.

In the position paper, spirituality and spiritual formation are discussed under four headings: "Spirituality in Light of the Lutheran Confessions;" "Christian Spirituality: Ecumenical Affirmations;" "The Shape of Spiritual Formation;" and "Spiritual Direction as Gospel Ministry." By and large the statement tends to focus on the *fides qua creditur* dimension of "spirituality" defining the term as "intentional practice of the Christian faith, both corporate and individual, insofar as it seeks to build up Christian identity and nurture 'life in the Spirit' in the multiple dimensions of personal existence." This emphasis on the practice of faith seems to hold true throughout the work. While theological beliefs and understandings regularly appear all through the writing (and the paper describes its task as "to engage and integrate the classical Christian tradition and the best contemporary resources in a theologically and pastorally responsible fashion"), theological beliefs and understandings are never explicitly defined as *fides quae creditur*, as a distinct, necessary, and essential part of spirituality itself. Instead theological beliefs and understandings seem to serve in an indicative, supportive, referential, demonstrative manner. I see this as a significant shortcoming.

The writers of the work state clearly that "[w]e have no Lutheran resources in spirituality which are not themselves already involved with wider Christian traditions of belief and practice. . . . Our task is to engage and integrate the classic Christian and the best contemporary resources in a theologically and pastorally responsible fashion." Remaining true to that theme, the paper does not raise up the centrality of theological beliefs to Lutheran spirituality (or as Hanson does, that Lutheran spirituality is distinct because of the foundational centrality of theological beliefs as such), but instead (and true to a clear intent of the reformers), places basic Lutheran spiritual beliefs such as sin, God's action in Jesus Christ, etc., under the canopy of ecumenical affirmations.

Spiritual formation is defined in the paper as "the work of the Spirit who brings us to Christ and joins our lives to his, so that in struggle and newness of life we bear the image of the crucified and risen Lord and make him known to the world." The last phrase of this sentence gives a positive spin to what Hanson describes as a shortcoming of Lutheran spirituality: the benign neglect of evangelism. Hansen puts it this way: "While today evangelism is a high priority among most Lutherans in developing nations, for the majority of Western Lutherans it is not" (Hansen 2000, 182). For a number of reasons, upon which I will not elaborate here, Lutherans historically have not seen evangelism as an essential part of spirituality.

The Southern Seminary statement also links spiritual formation closely to the sacraments of baptism and the Lord's supper, saying that "every Christian's personal discipline (which is implied and included in this understanding of formation) should be founded on the remembrance of Baptism, centered in Eucharistic worship, and reflect the normative pattern of Christian formation," and that "seminary students must receive the encouragement, urging, and instruction they need in order to find a stable and enlivening pattern of spiritual practice capable of sustaining them over the long haul in life and ministry."

I think it important and appropriate to mention here, an article written, quite proleptically, in 1980, by A. Roger Gobbel, then Professor of Communications and Education at Gettysburg Lutheran Seminary, entitled, "On Constructing Spirituality." Gobbel's article anticipates in many ways the understandings and emphases of the Southern Seminary position, especially in its focus on the Gospel and the remembrance of one's Baptism. He also includes an insightful and challenging section on the influence of cognitive development upon spirituality, a subject not covered in the Southern Seminary statement.

The position paper states further that "authentic spiritual direction is ecclesial ministry," that it is "a form of gospel ministry," and that it "needs to be defined and shaped in a theological context" (It is interesting that the importance of a theological context is explicated only here in the document.) A spiritual director is defined as "a Christian believer, ordained or not, who is called by God and the church to offer guidance and help to fellow-believers through the embodiment of God's word in close pastoral relationships of a special kind," and as "one called to accompany fellow-believers on the way of discipleship as a witness and speaker of the word of Christ." The statement goes on to say that "those [spiritual directors] who believe themselves called to this ministry should seek acknowledgement and confirmation of their call by the pastors and people of the church . . . need theological training," and "need spiritual direction."

Given the solidity with which the rest of the statement is crafted, the section on spiritual direction seems to display an uncertainty at most and a tentativeness and hesitancy at least about the official recognition and role of both the spiritual director and his/her functioning. This may reflect the present state of things regarding spiritual direction in this church today. In any case, I judge that this is the one part of the position paper that may require future development.

That the Two May Be One

As was stated above, the Southern Seminary position paper, in this writer's judgment at least, seems to exhibit a significant shortcoming. It does not explicitly include *fides quae creditur* as a distinct, necessary, and essential part of spirituality. This is an important omission, especially for Lutherans, given the discussion above.

The two dimensions of spirituality, especially as these have manifested themselves in the Lutheran tradition, call for seminary education to perform two essential tasks related to the spirituality and spiritual formation of persons preparing for pastoral ministries in the church. The first is the traditionally foundational task of bringing students into a critical and creative encounter with the formative, basic, and fundamental beliefs and understandings of the church as these are contained and expressed in its scriptures and in its historical, theological, practical, and pastoral traditions. The presentation and critical consideration of the faith of the church, the faith that one believes, the *fides quae creditur*, is an essential and necessary function of spiritual preparation in the Lutheran tradition. It ought to be explicitly understood as such, presented as such, and carried out as such. The second essential task complements the first and is integral to it. That task is to foster and cultivate the life of faith, one's living association with God, the *fides qua creditur*, again, in a critical and creative manner, and in a way that provides formative participation and guidance in the nurture and expression of the relationship established by God in one's baptism.

How these are to be accomplished has, is, and will be the subject of uncountable discussions, debates, papers and books. That they be accomplished, and that they be understood, presented, and accomplished together as two dimensions of one process is what is critical. The divided history of Lutheranism into pietist and orthodox camps, an unfortunate and sometimes destructive division which continues in various forms throughout our history and into the present day, and is part and parcel of the life of the seminary from which this is written, is one example of a divided spirituality, a spirituality which minimalizes either the content or the practice of faith, and cannot or will not undertake the discipline and labor involved in creatively and critically integrating the two dimensions of spirituality.

A recent email from one of my colleagues illustrates this. It is related to an incident in one of her classes in which a student exclaimed, "But we don't do anything spiritual here at the seminary." "Well!" the colleague wrote, "Let me just say we had a conversation!" It is in such conversations that the integrative glue for spirituality and spiritual formation is provided. Knowing this colleague, I'm sure that both the content and the living out of faith, and their necessary relationship, were part and parcel of the chat.

A Third Dimension

With this in mind, let me go now to what I see as a third, unique, and necessary dimension of Lutheran spirituality, one which has special relevance to this present discussion. It comes from Eric Gritsch. He calls that dimension "a liturgy of the mind." He derives it from Luther's understanding of and dedication to his academic vocation as a biblical theologian. Gritsch puts it this way.

> Luther became what he was because he followed his academic vocation. . . . Luther's unflinching commitment to his calling made him a pioneer of Christian thought and action. . . . To Luther, continuing theological education for the ordained as well as for the laity is a liturgy of the mind, a consistent rhythm of thinking 'gospel' in the midst of the temptation to think something else. . . . Like any other liturgy (from the Greek *leiturgia*, "the work of the people"), the liturgy of the mind requires intensive work and practice. Luther practiced it with monastic discipline every day of his life (Gritsch 1983).

What I understand Gritsch to be pointing to here is a third key component to be included in the nurturing and formation of ministerial spirituality, "a liturgy of the mind." "A liturgy of the mind" requires that one have a critical and creative understanding of the fundamentals of one's faith tradition and practice, and a life defining dedication to and appreciation for that tradition and practice. It also requires that one nurtures the capacity and willingness to use one's mind constantly and consistently to bring the fundamentals of that tradition and practice into critical, creative, and integrative conversation, not only with each other, but with all one encounters and does in the carrying out of one's ministerial vocation.

Writing from within the Lutheran tradition, Gritsch describes this as "a consistent rhythm of thinking 'gospel' in the midst of the temptation to think of something else" (Gritsch 1983). This integrative function is an essential component in both academic spiritual formation and in the practice of ministry. It requires a high degree of disciplined commitment and attention on the part of pastors, professors, and students. "A liturgy of the mind" is, in fact, a spiritual discipline and practice. It is also a necessary prelude to responsibly differentiated and informed ethical/moral understanding, deliberation, and action in pastoral ministry.

A Three-legged Stool

Martha Stortz, a Lutheran ethicist with an informed and demonstrated interest in spiritual formation, uses the metaphor of "a three-legged stool" to describe Luther's approach to spirituality and spiritual formation, naming the legs of the stool as "worship, catechesis, and individual prayer" (Stortz 1998, 62, 63). The metaphor is an accurate, creative, and useful one. It implies a necessary integrative strength and balance among the three legs if the stool is to stand well. I would like to adapt that metaphor, with some appropriate modification, to our discussion of spirituality, spiritual formation, and preparation for pastoral ministry. I would like to suggest that those of us who participate vocationally in the spirituality and spiritual formation of persons preparing for vocations in ministry also consider a three-legged approach. However, in this case, the legs would include the teaching and nurturing of a faith that one believes, the teaching and nurturing of a faith by which one both relationally cultivates and lives out one's beliefs, and, the teaching and nurturing of a liturgy of the mind.

A Polyphonic Postscript

Allow me to present one additional and quite personal image related to spirituality, spiritual formation, and preparation for pastoral ministry. The image comes from Dietrich Bonhoeffer. It was included in one of his *Letters and Papers from Prison*, written while he was imprisoned by the Nazis at Tegel Prison in Berlin for his participation in a plot to assassinate Hitler. The image is a musical one: "polyphony." It speaks to my spiritual consciousness because a central portion of my own spirituality was formed musically, in this case during my undergraduate college years by the discipline and joy of both learning and singing the great choral music of the Lutheran and Western Christian traditions.[1] My intent and hope is that the image might speak also, in a heart-and-mind inspiring fashion, to those who read this chapter.

> God requires that we should love him eternally with our hearts, yet not so as to compromise or diminish our earthly affections, but as a kind of *cantus firmus* to which the other melodies of life provide the counterpoint. Earthly affection is one of these contrapuntal themes, a theme which enjoys an autonomy of its own. . . . Where the ground bass is firm and clear, there is nothing to stop the counterpoint from being developed to the utmost of its limits. Both ground bass and counterpoint are "without confusion and yet distinct," in the words of the Calcedonian formula, like Christ in his divine and human natures. Perhaps the importance of polyphony in music lies in the fact that it is a musical reflection of this Christological fact, and that it is therefore an essential element in the Christian life. . . .We must have a good clear *cantus firmus*. Without it there can be no full or perfect sound, but with it the counterpoint has a firm support and cannot get out of tune or fade out, yet is always a perfect whole in its own right. Only a polyphony of this kind can give life a wholeness, and at the same time assure us that nothing can go wrong so long as the *cantus firmus* is kept going (Bonhoeffer 1953, 99, 100).

References

Benne, Robert. 1998. "Lutheran Ethics: Perennial Themes and Contemporary Challenges." Pages 11-30 in *The Promise of Lutheran Ethics*. Edited by Karen L. Bloomquist and John R. Stumme. Minneapolis: Fortress Press.

Bonhoeffer, Dietrich. 1953. *Letters and Papers from Prison*. London: S.C.M. Press.

Braaten, Carl E. and Robert W. Jenson, eds. 1998. *Union with Christ: The New Finnish Interpretation of Luther*. Minneapolis: Fortress Press.

Broadway, Bill. 2001. "Good for the Soul—and the Bottom Line: Firms Promote Spirituality in Workplace and Find It Pays." *The Washington Post*, 19 August:A1.

Gerkin, Charles V. 1997. *An Introduction to Pastoral Care*. Nashville: Abingdon Press.

Gobbel, A. Roger. 1980. "On Constructing Spirituality." *Religious Education* 75/4:409-21.

Gritsch, Eric W. 1983. "Luther: The Power of Vocation." *The Circle*. October.

Hanson, Bradley. 2000. *A Graceful Life: Lutheran Spirituality for Today*. Minneapolis: Fortress Press.

Hoffman, Bengt R. 2003. *Theology of the Heart: The Role of Mysticism in the Theology of Martin Luther*. Minneapolis: Kirk House Publishers.

Holifield, E. Brooks. 1983. *A History of Pastoral Care in America*. Nashville: Abingdon Press.

Hunter, Rodney J. 1998. "Religious Caregiving in a Postmodern Context: Recovering Ecclesia." *Journal of Pastoral Theology* 8:15-27.

Lundborg, Paul S. 1991. "Spiritual Formation: An Ancient Practice for Lutheran Parish Life Today." D. Min. dissertation/project, San Francisco Theological Seminary.

Luther, Martin. 1529. "The Large Catechism." Pages 377-480 in *The Book of Concord*. Edited by Robert Kolb and Timothy J. Wengert. Minneapolis: Fortress Press. 2000.

_____. 1535. "A Simple Way to Pray." Pages 193-211 in *Luther's Works*, vol 43. Edited by Gustav K. Wienke. Philadelphia: Fortress Press. 1968.

_____. 1537. "The Smalcald Articles." Pages 295-328 in *The Book of Concord*. Edited by Robert Kolb and Timothy J. Wengert. Minneapolis: Fortress Press, 2000.

_____. 1539. "Preface to the Wittenberg Edition of Luther's German Writings." Pages 63-68 in *Martin Luther's Basic Theological Writings*. Edited by Timothy F. Lull. Minneapolis: Fortress Press, 1989.

Lutheran Theological Southern Seminary Faculty. 1998. "Spirituality and Spiritual Formation: A Position Paper of the Faculty of Lutheran Theological Southern Seminary." Columbia: LTSS.

McNeill, John T. 1965. *A History of the Cure of Souls.* New York: Harper and Row.

Oberman, Heiko A. 1994. *The Reformation: Roots and Ramifications.* Grand Rapids: William B. Eerdmans.

Stortz, Martha. 1998. "Practicing Christians: Prayer as Formation." Pages 55-73 in *The Promise of Lutheran Ethics.* Edited by Karen L. Bloomquist and John R. Stumme. Minneapolis: Fortress Press

Vaillant, George. 2002. *Aging Well: Surprising Guideposts to a Happier Life from The Landmark Harvard Study of Adult Development.* Boston: Little Brown and Company.

Wentz, Abdel Ross. 1964. *A Basic History of Lutheranism in America.* Philadelphia: Fortress Press.

Wuthnow, Robert. 2003. "The Changing Nature of Work in the United States: Implications for Vocation, Ethics, and Faith." *The Cresset* 671: 5-13.

Luther, Lutherans, and Spirituality[2]

Kirsi Stjerna

What is Lutheran spirituality? While not trying to offer a definite description, I want to look at the central elements rising from Luther's teachings as the foundation for what we could name as the characteristics of specifically Lutheran spirituality. I will name some of these points against the background of Martin Luther's spiritual journey and the 16th century reformation of spirituality. In so doing, I will introduce new insights from the Finnish scholars whose interpretation of Luther's understanding of justification is highly relevant to a discussion on the basics and uniqueness of Lutheran spirituality. I hope that the vision discussed in this article helps the reader to appreciate the peculiar nature of Lutheran spirituality, its theological articulation and foundation, and its flexibility and universality in application.

The term "spirituality," as Alistair McGrath's points out in his *A Christian Spirituality* (1999), "is resistant to precise definition," but we could say that spirituality in general "concerns the quest for a fulfilled and authentic religious life, involving the bringing together of the ideas distinctive of that religion and the whole experience of living on the basis of and within the scope of that religion" (McGrath 1999, 2). Christian spirituality is a variation of that, with its concern for "authentic Christian existence "within the scope of the Christian faith" (ibid.). "Spirituality is the outworking in real life of a person's religious faith—what a person does with what they believe. It is not just about ideas, although the basic ideas of the Christian faith are important to Christian spirituality. It is about the way in which Christian life is conceived and lived (ibid.). Spirituality, we could say, is a fundamental dimension of human life. Luther, I believe, would agree with this.

Luther would agree as well with Mark McIntosh who, in his work, *Mystery of Faith* (2000), describes theology/living theologically in a way that we could describe as living spiritually: "theology is about seeing the meaning of things in the context of life with God." Theology is about seeking out and listening to that meaning, hearing it not just as any kind of meaning but as God's meaning. . . .What does your life mean as it takes place moment by moment in the presence of God" (McIntosh 2000, 2). Luther has said that one becomes a theologian by living and dying (WA 5; 163, 28). We could develop that thought further and argue theologically that spirituality is about living and dying with a meaning.

In the past the confessionally and doctrinally oriented Lutherans have discussed theological issues much more than spiritual concerns—without intending a split there but nevertheless being less comfortable about proceeding in discourse from theology to spirituality, from the abstract to the concrete and personal. Now the situation compels Lutherans to react as a plethora of non-Christian or non-Lutheran spiritualities are being embraced by people hungry for spiritual direction or "identity." Lutherans need to define what "Lutheran spirituality" might be and what unique meanings it has to offer to people today.

Since in the last five hundred years or so "Lutheran" has come to mean something slightly different than "Luther-an," I begin with comments on Luther's theological search for authentic spirituality. Martin Luther (1483-1546), a medieval monk, was passionate about God. He wanted to perfect the medieval monastic way of spiritual life. His passion was to find a merciful God and the certainty of forgiveness, and the *vita spiritualis* that had been practiced by the monastics for centuries seemed the most assured path to spiritual perfection. He tried, overachieved in his ambition, and failed. Or so he felt.

His rescue came from the (Pauline) "gospel experience": his new insight that one does not become holy and spiritual by good intentions or works, by doing "what is in us." He was relieved to admit that we have nothing to offer to God, just the Old Adam and Eve—a horribly ugly sinner. Reading Paul (Rom 1:17) gave him the realization that one is justified, made right with God and holy by faith alone, by Christ who as *maximus peccator* has taken on himself all the dirt and sin and gives himself totally to the baptized children of God.[3] What was fresh in Luther's realization was his profoundly experienced recognition of human fallibility and corruption, and his absolute, child-like trust in the mystery of God's grace and saving will. With the slogan, "Christ alone/faith alone/grace alone," he preached about holiness and spirituality as something other than ambition and perfection preserved for select individuals or groups. He made a fundamental discovery that God need not be sought further than in one's own life, from one's daily reality. His insight was that Christ is already there, in faith, through the Word, as effected by God the Holy Spirit through the Word. Luther was convinced that God is where the Word is, and the Word has come to us and comes to us as we proclaim the Word. With these realizations, intellectual as well as deeply existential, Luther's entire life changed. And the church would change, or split, with him.[4]

One concrete consequence of this spiritual discovery was his leaving his monastic cell and celibate "angelic" life. Luther's view of spiritual life became remarkably egalitarian. "Normal," ordinary life became the every man and every woman's monastery, chapel, the spiritual realm where one expresses and appropriates one's faith. Luther's personal shift from monastic life to family life is a significant milestone and speaks to his discovery about the limitlessness of the spiritual realm: in God's creation, everything and everybody is holy and with a holy purpose—doing the house chores is as holy as presiding at worship or reading devotions. Even sexuality is good, a source of blessing rather than a curse burning in human flesh. Luther saw motherhood/parenthood as a particularly sacred vocation, an aspect of life he came to know first-hand as a father of six children (not counting the adopted and foster children).

Speaking of Luther's marriage, for women the Reformation's sanctification of marital and sexual life was potentially very good news, indicating at least a more positive affirmation of womanhood and humanness, as well as intimate human relations. No longer did a woman need to look for spiritual fulfillment and calling exclusively inside the monastery walls, or from extreme forms of asceticism, but she could embrace another path, such as parenthood and domestic work. That said, with the "loss" of the monastic option, women did indeed lose a significant choice, the choice not to become mothers and wives so as to be free to concentrate on spiritual and intellectual development in the all female environment of a convent (even if generally under the supervision of monks); they lost a "room of their own" and their theological/spiritual voice outside their homes. This aspect was of course beyond our 16th century reformer's scope of understanding. We could hardly call him the liberator of women. He did not want to become anybody's liberator in a social/cultural sense; his liberation was about liberation from religious oppression and burdened consciences. His concern was gender-neutral: the salvation and spiritual well being of men and women, and children (his great concern).[5]

Luther's marital experiences naturally enhanced his (for his time) exceptionally inclusive view of the sacredness of life in different vocations, and of the blessedness of "ordinary" ways of serving God. With a pleasant domestic experience in his personal life, Luther placed a noticeable emphasis on home as the starting point for a spiritual journey. Luther emphasized the need for the domestic education of all the baptized. Historically, women (not ordained) would excel in this realm as those who actually instilled the new faith in the new little Lutherans; they were the professors and pastors of domestic academies. Luther's *Small Catechism* is a timeless testimony to Luther's fatherly concern to educate the entire family, and to provide tools for good spiritual habits and Christian living, that is, life based on ardent continuous prayer, the habit of daily "eating" of the Scripture and meditating, regular receiving of the Sacrament, intentional service to others, and other catechetic principles (see Peura 2000).

Reformation of Spirituality

Scott Hendrix writes in his essay on Luther's "guestly" spirituality: "If spirituality is taken in the sense of piety or living the Christian life, then I am convinced that Luther initiated a reformation of spirituality; or, to say it another way: the reformation which Luther initiated was also intended to be a reformation of spirituality. Luther and the evangelical movement proposed to change the actual pattern of Christian living and they urged that pattern upon the faithful as the genuine way of being spiritual, as authentic Christian spirituality" (Hendrix 1999, 250). Luther was not about to found a new church, but "from the beginning he did intend to establish a new spirituality" (Hendrix 1999, 252). New theology "happened" as it was needed to justify and explain changes in spiritual practices and traditions (ibid., 253). The Reformation was about reformation of spirituality, reformation of practices of piety, reformation of tools that sustain spiritual living and theological living.[6]

On the basis of Luther's doctrine of "justification by faith alone" and "union with Christ," we can say with Hendrix that "[t]he spiritual life in Christ is for Luther not just a possibility but in some sense a present reality." When we live a Christian life and do the things that belong to Christian life—"baptize, preach, console, exhort, work, and suffer"—Christ is the one who actually does these things (ibid., 256, 254). In other words, we are living spiritual lives when we are living in Christ, which happens by the power of God's Spirit in daily living.

Simo Peura from Finland, through his close reading of Luther, has concluded that some of the Lutheran Confessions differ from Luther in explaining the kind of new spiritual reality that justification by faith brings about. Peura has some provocative thoughts on this. He says: "Because of the Formula of Concord and the neo-Kantian interpretation of Luther, gift and the effective aspect of justification have lost their ontological content in Lutheran theology. . . The content of gift is actually reduced to the Christian's insight that he[she] has a new position *coram deo*" (Peura 1998, 46).

> In my opinion, the FC [Formula of Concord] and modern Lutheran theology have not correctly communicated Luther's view of grace and gift. . . . Justification

includes gift in its broader sense, that is, in its effective aspect as the renewal of the sinner (renovatio). This aspect belongs integrally to Luther's view of justification, and it is not a mere consequence of forensic imputation. God changes the sinner ontologically in the sense that he or she participates in God and in his [God's] divine nature, being made righteous and 'a god.' This interpretation is based on the thesis that both grace and gift are a righteousness given in Christ to a Christian. This donation presupposes that Christ is really present and that he indwells the Christian" (ibid., 48).

Peura argues further that "Luther's view of salvation includes ideas of participation in God and divinization. Both aspects of justification, imputed righteousness as well as effective, transforming righteousness, are based on the indwelling of Christ within us and our participation in Him" (Peura 2000, 30).

For Peura, if justification means becoming one with God, it also means "being made holy," an expression explicitly used in the Catechism. How and when do we become holy, what does it mean theologically and in practice? Finnish Luther scholarship, with its attention to Luther's use of the concept "theosis" when talking about the new reality of the "justified person" and of consequent holy living, is worth paraphrasing here because it may radically shape our discussion of Lutheran theology of holiness and spirituality.

Finnish Luther research
on the holiness of union with Christ

Finnish Luther scholars argue that Luther indeed speaks of a new reality when he talks about the life of the justified by faith. Thus, as Hendrix says, "Finnish scholarship has performed a service by calling attention again to the new reality in Christ which constituted the heart of Luther's spirituality" (Hendrix 1999, 258). The key concept leading to these stimulating conclusions is the idea of *theosis*, divinization, which the Finnish Luther "school" has claimed to be a central motif in different loci of Luther's theology and at the heart of the doctrine of justification.

Tuomo Mannermaa stated his vision first in *In Ipsa Fide Christus Adest* (1978), a book that resulted from his participation in the Lutheran and Orthodox ecumenical dialogue (which Mannermaa admits as the outer impulse for his research). His claim that "[t]he idea of divine life in Christ who is really present in faith lies at the very center of the theology of the Reformer" has been supported by several dissertations, some already published and some still forthcoming (Mannermaa 1988, 2). While this perspective has been recognized as theologically important as a challenge to older schools of Luther scholarship, it is equally important to realize the importance of this perspective for understanding the theological foundation of Lutheran spirituality.

Against earlier Luther research, Mannermaa and his "school" argue that the concept of participation in God (*theosis*), unification with God, is inherent in and fundamental for Luther's theology. To counter the suspicion among international scholars regarding the appropriateness of the term *theosis* for Luther, Simo Peura (1998, 51) has found significant evidence in Luther for the idea of *theosis* as "deification" or "God's indwelling or inhabitation" in the human being. Luther explicitly states that "a Christian is a god, God's child and infinite, because God indwells in him [her]" (WA 4:280, 2-5). Simply stated, for Luther "deification means for the Christian participation in God and in his [God's] divine nature" (WA 3:106, 14-15).

A brief summary of the arguments made by Finns around the concept of *theosis* will hopefully explain the basis and ramifications of this radical thought. According to Mannermaa, in Luther's theology

> *[t]heosis* is based causally on the divinity of God. . . . The theosis of the believer is initiated when God bestows on the believer God's essential properties.
>
> Before God gives himself [sic] to a person in his Word (which is God himself), he performs his "nihilizing work"—he makes the person "empty" and "nothing." This *reductio in nihilum*, of course, does not imply a total annihilation of the person. It refers only to the destruction of the individual's constant effort to make himself god and to justify himself [sic].
>
> One must pass through this agony and, ultimately, through the cross in order to achieve a true *cognitio sui*.

Only in this way is one made *vacuum* and *capax Dei*. And this doctrine implies that, according to Luther, the modus of a Christian is always *passio*: a person is neither inwardly nor outwardly active; one experiences only what God affects in him or her.

Luther's concept of *theosis*, then, is understood correctly only in connection with his theology of the cross. The participation that is a real part of his theology is hidden under its opposite, the *passio* through which one is emptied. It is not grasped in rational knowledge but only in faith, and the grasp that faith has of it in this life is still only the beginning of a much greater participation that awaits in eschatological fulfillment.

God gives himself as the Word in the historical birth of Christ and the spiritual birth of Christ in the faith of the believer (Mannermaa 1998, 10).[8]

In other words, Mannermaa argues that "[t]he right relationship of faith is not a striving, dynamic movement of love toward the transcendent. God cannot be found 'above' by means of striving love. Rather, he [God] is 'below' in faith, present in the sinful human. . ." (Mannermaa 1998, 15). One becomes rapt beyond oneself in God, because of Christ who lives in one in faith. In faith one participates in God's being and, thus, in love.

This explanation of what happens in and as a result of justification, which is the key Lutheran doctrine and perspective, describes the faith-based, grace-initiated God-human relationship as a mystical union that is real, personal and effected by the Word. Justification understood as the human being made one with God as a result of God entering one's life in faith implies a totally different way of looking at the theological vision for spirituality, life with the Spirit, than if justification were only understood to be about external forgiveness. Exclusive focus on preaching external forgiveness and imputed righteousness—as a state of "not-guilty"—bolstered with Lutheran teaching on the bondage of the will and general human inability in godly matters provides very few bridges or tools for speaking about life with God as a reality that is personal and somehow transforming ontologically. Seeing justification as an act of being made holy and one with God opens logically and naturally many more ways of seeing how spirituality is lived and articulated in Lutheran context, for it enables one to deal with the question of what justification and faith mean in real life and in one's ontological and personal relation to God.

Mannermaa, thus, highlights in Luther a "radically different concept of the relationship between God and [the hu]man than had been previously described in the interpretative traditions of the Luther Renaissance and of dialectical theology" (Mannermaa 1998, 11-12). Offering a new take on Luther's epistemology and ontological philosophy, Mannermaa writes about the "essence of the relationship to God" as "a community of being" (Mannermaa 1998, 5-6, 12). To explain this community of being, or union, he argues that "God is in *relation* to him[God]self in the movement of Word (*Deum Patrem sibi suum apud se verbum proferre*) at the same time that he[God] *is* this movement of the Word. . . .This understanding of the being of God is the basis for understanding the being-present-of-Christ in faith" (ibid., 12). Divinization of the human being, thus, results from this movement of God towards us in the Word, who is Christ. As Luther writes in his "Sermo de duplici iustitiae 1518": "Thus the righteousness of Christ becomes our righteousness through faith in Christ, and everything that is his, even he himself, becomes ours, and he who believes in Christ clings to Christ and is one with Christ and has the same righteousness with him" (Mannermaa 1986, 6).[9]

In Mannermaa's view, this idea of participation is the key for understanding different loci in Luther's theology, and I would add that it is also central in terms of spirituality. Clearly, the idea presupposes a certain understanding of Christ's presence. As Mannermaa and Peura point out, "Luther does not distinguish between the person and the work of Christ. . . . Christ is both *favor* of God (forgiveness of sins, atonement, abolition of wrath) and gift (*donum*), God himself present. Faith means justification precisely on the basis of Christ's person being present in it as favor and gift. *In ipsa fide Christus adest*: in faith itself Christ is present, and so the whole of salvation" (ibid., 14-15). Ultimately this view is quite mystical, for it recognizes Christ as being personally present in the believer, rather than merely his benefits. Faith in this view also is more than an abstract virtue. It is a reality-changing instrument that unites the divine and the human, ontologically.

Faith is central to Luther's spirituality. *"In ipsa fide Christus adest"* could be the motto of Luther's/Luther-an spirituality. A motto that reminds us of the fact that holiness comes from outside, from God, and is not ours because of our deeds, but is a given, a gift, and only then becomes ours as it brings God to us.

What, then, of the concept of love? How could one talk about spirituality without the concept that has been such a central part of Christian teaching on spirituality and which, in many ways, is generally seen as the fulfillment of law in the biblical sense? In Luther's view, I would argue, faith does not exclude love or make it unnecessary. Quite the contrary, love is an intrinsic part of the life of faith, of spiritual living, the manifestation and realization of one's faith-relationship to God. Loving follows "naturally" and necessarily from being justified by faith. In the Lutheran view, love is not seen as a virtue or a deed or anything that brings "merit" but is rather a natural response to grace as the way of living a Christian life—while struggling with one's ability to initiate and sustain good. One could say that the Christian's ability to love, in Luther's view, is based on God' own being, love, in which the human being participates in faith. Love, in Luther's theology, is something that results from the reality of being made one with God and part of the community of being with the Divine, who is love.

In other words, one could say that divinization, becoming "one with God," is what generates love in the believer. "Divinization means our union with Christ and our transformation into God's love. . . .Through faith we Christians are in union with Christ, we participate in Christ, we are made righteous, and we are deified, in order that we may love God and our neighbours" (Peura 2000, 31). In addition to this theological insight, Luther, in his Catechisms, is also able to explain what loving God and one's neighbor entails in real life.

As Mannermaa explains further, for Luther "[f]aith means participation in the being and thus in the properties of God. And one of the properties. . . is love. Christ, who is present in faith as *donum*, brings love with him [God] . . . and God is love"

(Mannermaa 1998, 16). Faith imparts love, which is indeed the fulfillment of the law (ibid., 16-18). In other words, justification by faith liberates one to love, which is the necessary actualization of faith without which there is no spiritual, holy living. And as in faith, so also in love, Christ is the real subject, the source, the incarnated *agape* in whom we participate in faith. I would characterize this Christ-induced love as "alien," in the same way that Luther sees justifying faith and righteousness as "alien." As Luther says: "Christus manet in me et ista vita vivit in me, et vita quo vivo, est Christus" [Christ remains in me, and that life lives in me, and the life through which I live is Christ.] (WA 40 I, 283, 7-9; Mannermaa 1998, 18-19).

Thus, from a Lutheran perspective the Golden Rule has a central role in spirituality (Raunio 1993). The Golden Rule also happens to be at the heart of what *theosis* entails in a Christian's life as a justified person. As Luther articulates in his "On Christian Freedom," a result of Christ living in a Christian is that Christians are free through faith from everything but bound by love to everything. Luther says: "We conclude, therefore, that a Christian lives not in himself [sic], but in Christ and his neighbor. Otherwise he is not a Christian. He lives in Christ through faith, in his neighbor through life. By faith he is caught up beyond himself into God. By love he descends beneath himself into his neighbor. Yet he always remains in God and in his[sic] love" (LW 31: 371; Mannermaa 1998, 19). Here, in my view, is the "meaning" offered by Lutheran spirituality.

Characteristics of Lutheran Spirituality

On the basis of Luther's central insights and the new reading of Luther's notion of *theosis*, and on the basis of what has been central in Lutheran teaching and preaching, we could identify the following six principles that characterize "Luther-an" spirituality and theology of spiritual living:

1. Luther's/Lutheran spirituality is God-centered: it is based in the belief in the triune God, while it is Christ-centric with its emphasis on justification by faith because of Christ. The notion of the role of the Holy Spirit is interwoven with the theology of how God works in human life through Word and Sacraments, while pneumatology is otherwise articulated less

explicitly than one would expect given the emphasis on grace. In the Lutheran view, the new spiritual reality, the new birth and life that comes with justification, is not possible without the Spirit who "holy-fies."[10] As Hendrix says, "The essence of Luther's spirituality, connectedness with Christ, is a work of the Holy Spirit, who creates that connection through baptism and the Word" (1999, 260). The Holy Spirit mediates between the sinner and Christ, helping the Christian to become one with Christ. "[T]he Holy Spirit brings our union with Christ into existence and produces in us love for God" (Peura 2000, 29). Obviously, there is no spirituality without or apart from the Spirit.

2. More distinctively, Lutheran spirituality is faith-centered. Faith is "Luther's main idea to explain what God is, what God has done for us, and what God is doing for us, i.e. how the word of God becomes a reality of our life." Furthermore, "[t]he real faith is not a *fides absoluta* but a *fides incarnata*" (Peura 2000, 17). Faith is the link between God and the believer, and the notion of the gift nature of this faith draws on the Lutheran emphasis on spirituality as being God-centered, and God-initiated, and as such Word-centered.

3. As faith centered, Lutheran spirituality is essentially Word-centered; everything relies on God's promise and the Word as the means of bringing Christ to human life. God comes to us in Word. The *unio cum Deo* occurs when Christ is proclaimed (WA 9:439-42; Peura 1998, 53, note 21). The Word brings the Spirit who evokes the faith that joins one with God.[11]

4. Lutheran spirituality as Word-centered is also thoroughly sacramental as it emphasizes the vital role of baptism and Eucharist as the concrete gifts mediating Christ and God's grace to us. As Simo Peura says, according to Luther, "union with Christ is effected in baptism. The necessary precondition of baptism is always the preaching of God's word. The sacrament of baptism achieves validity when the Word of God, that is, Christ, joins himself to natural water" (Peura 1998, 53). Another external means of new birth and sustenance of holy life is the Lord's Supper: in the Lutheran view Christ is there in real presence and united with those who receive Christ in the Word. These means are used effectively in a Christian community where the Holy Spirit works through Word and sacraments. Thus, Lutheran

spirituality is also communal and fellowship-oriented. Spirituality is fostered, nurtured and expressed in communion with others in the community of believers, which begins at home and continues in the worshiping community.

5. In its principles, Lutheran spirituality is radically egalitarian and inclusive, as is illustrated not only by the central doctrine of justification by faith, but also by the principle of the priesthood of all believers/baptized. As Peura says, Luther "neglected . . . the distinction between ordinary Christians and religious specialists" (2000, 15). The very Lutheran teaching of the priesthood of all believers speaks about the Lutheran view of the sacred in created life, of trust in God's immanence in the midst of the mundane, including all vocations and all human beings. This supports the premise that spirituality is not reserved for the few and elect but is an aspect—or nerve—of the life of all human beings.

6. Lutheran spirituality is catechetic and family-centered. Luther's *Small Catechism* is the primary source of and for Lutheran spirituality. Historically, catechism is taught at home and in the church community, in word and in example. As a teaching and confessing tool of Lutheran faith, the *Small Catechism* has served as a timelessly applicable *summa* of Lutheran theology with practical, pedagogical directives for building spiritual habits (such as regular reading and meditating on the Bible, regular praying, concentrated reflection, and "decent," honorable daily living etc.)[12]

7. Lutheran spirituality has one more aspect that is more peculiar and has been less widely recognized thus far: the mystical aspect. The very Lutheran idea of justification by faith and its realization in personal union with Christ, in *theosis*, participation in divine love which leads to holy living, allow us to re-visit the word that is loaded in meaning. Obviously, Luther was not a mystic like Meister Eckhart or Julian of Norwich or others in the Western mystical tradition, but there are enough connecting points between the theological insights and ultimate concerns of the mystics and of Luther to argue for a mystical dimension in Luther's/Luther-an spirituality. Though this is not an entirely new idea, it is only now gaining broader appreciation.

The late Professor Bengt Hoffman, a Swede who ended his career at the Lutheran Theological Seminary at Gettysburg, is one of those who paid attention to Luther's mystical side even at a time when it was not scholarly advantageous to do so. He pointed out the clear emphasis in Luther's theology on "Christ in us" and spoke about the the "inextricably joined inner and outer sides of faith," going thus against the predominant Lutheran "confessional" stress on the idea of Christ and justification for us (Hoffman 1976, 326; see Hendrix 1999, 260). In his works, he not only challenges a long tradition of Luther-research but also Western academic disciplines that "have been molded by epistemologies based on an immanental, mechanistic view of knowledge" (Hoffman 1984, 77). In his criticism of Western epistemologies and readings of Luther, he calls attention to "a knowing by spiritual experience, a knowing-in-Christ" (Hoffman 1984, 78).[13] Luther, according to Hoffman, spoke of "*sapientia experimentalis* as he propounded the meaning of justification" (Hoffman 1984, 86).[14]

Hoffman says: ". . . we find a strong mystical, that is subjective, private, personal element in Luther's faith. . . . We need to distinguish between different types of mystical experience" (Hoffman 1976, 322). He quotes Erwin Iserloh who "asserts that there was in Luther's theology a 'continuous mystical approach' coinciding with this deepest religious experience." "But we have to take more seriously the fact that Luther until his dying day spoke—sometimes in changed terminology—the language of mystical theology as an integral part of or as a necessary counterpoint to the language of objective faith" (Hoffman 1976, 322). Hoffmann reminds readers of Luther's definition of mysticism: "Mystical theology is experience of God."[15] And that experience was central to Luther and his theology, as observed also by Heiko Oberman: "Mysticism is not simply one locus in Luther's theology but its very foundation" (Hoffman 1984, 84).

While pointing to the fact that in Luther's theology we can see a manifest interest in the "inner side," the experiential and experimental side of faith, "combined with the 'inner' side of God's gift: justification by faith in Christ," Hoffman also cautions the reader that Luther was "aware of the extremely subjective. His interest in a number of medieval mystics was always balanced by his emphasis on 'the external Word.'" (Hoffman 1998, 27, 18). Luther's words on "righteousness outside us" and "Christ for us" were not just phrases for Luther but expressed his personal experience and "consciousness of faith." When he talked about God's indwelling and residing in one's heart, using the words "to feel" and "to experience," Luther was "not speaking objectively. He spoke from experience" (ibid., 18-19, 21, 23).

It is significant to notice that, according to Hoffman, and I agree, "Luther never treated 'mysticism' as a uniform belief system nor as having one connotation." Furthermore, "[i]f the terms 'mysticism,' 'mystical,' and 'mystics' can in any way be applied to Luther's theology, and to Luther himself, one must come to an agreement that they embrace the non-rational, experiential aspect. The experiential played a major role in the theology of the reformer" (ibid., 20). Luther "did not have much interest in mysticism as an '-ism', as a composite of ideas that has to be accepted or rejected. He spoke about mysticism as the inner side of the external confession. . . . And mystical theology, for Luther, is about experience of God" (ibid., 21). I would say that at the heart of Luther's theology is his conviction and experience of justification by faith as union with God. I would say that it is fair to call this "mystical."

Hoffman's thesis and attempts to reconcile mysticism with Luther/Lutheran have been criticized, rejected, and found again recently. Especially in light of Finnish Luther research, Hoffman's arguments find new support and invite a promising re-examination of the principles and depths of Lutheran spirituality, drawing on Luther's Word-based and experience-based God-centered theology of grace, especially prominent in the doctrine of justification.[16]

Bernard McGinn's definition of mysticism is helpful here—even if he probably would not count Luther among the mystics in a classic sense of the word. He says, "The mystical element within Christianity involved a form of immediate encounter with God whose essential purpose is to convey a loving knowledge . . . that transforms the mystic's consciousness and whole way of life" (Hendrix 1999, 261, note 4; McGimm 1996). Luther's theology does not fit the description perfectly as he did not use the language of transformed consciousness or enlightened mystical knowledge in describing the ultimate goal of the soul's union with God. Instead, he spoke of the immediate, real, personal encounter and union with God—in the Word! He speaks of this often and passionately, totally convinced that he is talking about a new reality, not about an ideal; he explains the mystery of justification and its importance and reality time after time, but eventually does not fully explain the nature of the union and how exactly it happens. He leaves it what it is, mystical, as is the work of the Word—mystical.

Luther, like any true mystic, acknowledges the human soul's ultimate dependency on God and God's action, an experience one comes to after being emptied of all self-confidence and vain glory. The goal for Luther and the mystics, generally speaking, is similar, though the path leading to the goal is explained differently, due to different understandings of free will and the possibilities of human-divine collaboration. We could safely call Luther a Word-mystic and recognize that there are elements in his spirituality and theology that resonate with the Christian mystics who have gone before or after him. His theology and experience of the Word are so crucial that we could even describe Luther's, as well as Lutheran, spirituality as Word-spirituality.

Luther expresses his theological vision for Word-spirituality in a sermon from 1525. "We are filled with God, and he pours into us all his gifts and grace and fills us with his spirit. . . .His [God's] life lives in us . . . his love causes love to arise in us. . . . He fills us in order that everything that He is and everything He can do might be in us in all its fullness, and work powerfully, so that we might be divinized throughout—not having only a small part of God, or merely some parts of Him, but having all his fullness. . . . What must be done instead is to show the right and straight way to your being filled with God, so that you do not lack any part but have it all gathered together, and so that all you say, all you think and everywhere you go—in sum, all your life— is throughout divine" (WA 4:280, 2-5; also WA 3:106, 14-15; Peura 2000, 30).]

References

Selected texts from Luther. Including, Heidelberg Disputation (1518), On Two Kinds of Righteousness (1519), The Freedom of a Christian (1520), LW 31: 39-58, 31:297-306, 31:333-377; Small and Large Catechism (1529), in *The Book of Concord*, ed. Robert Kolb and Timothy Wengert, Minneapolis: Fortress Press, 2000.

Braaten, Carl E., and Robert W. Jenson, eds. 1998. *Union With Christ: The New Finnish Interpretation of Luther*. Grand Rapids, Michigan/Cambridge, U.K.: William B. Eerdmans Publishing Company.

Hendrix, Scott. 1999. "Martin Luther's Reformation of Spirituality." *Lutheran Quarterly* 13/3: 249-270.

Hoffman, Bengt R. 1975. "On the Relationship Between Mystical Faith and Moral life in Luther's Thought." *Gettysburg Seminary Bulletin* 55:21-35.

Hoffman, Bengt R. 1976. *Luther and the Mystics: A Re-examination of Luther's Spiritual Experiences and His Relationship to the Mystics*. Minneapolis: Augsburg Publishing House.

Hoffman, Bengt R. 1984. "The Present Significance of Mysticism to the Christian Faith." Pages 75-87 in *Elevatis Oculis: Festschrift in Honorem Seppo A. Teinonen, Prof. of Systematic Theology*. Helsinki, Vammala: Gummerus.

Hoffman, Bengt R. 1998. *Theology of the Heart: The Role of Mysticism in the Theology of Martin Luther*. Edited by Pearl Willemssen Hoffman. Minneapolis: Kirk House Publishers.

Mannermaa, Tuomo. 1978. *In Ipsa Fide Christus Adest*. Helsinki: Missiologian Seuran Julkaisuja.

Mannermaa, Tuomo. 1997. "Participation And Love in the Theology of Martin Luther." Pages 303-311 in *Philosophical Studies in Religion, Metaphysics, and Ethics: Essay in Honour of Heikki Kirjavainen*. Edited by Tuomo Mannermaa. Helsinki: Luther-Agricola-Gesellschaft.

Mannermaa, Tuomo. 1998. "Justification and Theosis in Lutheran-Orthodox Perspective." Pages 25-41 in *Union With Christ: The New Finnish Interpretation of Luther*. Edited by Carl E. Braaten and Robert W. Jenson. Grand Rapids, Michigan/Cambridge, U.K.: William B. Eerdmans Publishing Company.

Mannermaa, Tuomo. 1998. "The Doctrine of Justification and Christology. Chapter A, Section One of the Christ Present in Faith." *Concordia Theological Quarterly* 54/3:206-239.

Mannermaa, Tuomo. 1998. "Why Is Luther So Fascinating?" Pages 1-20 in *Union With Christ: The New Finnish Interpretation of Luther*. Edited by Carl E. Braaten and Robert W. Jenson. Grands Rapids, Michigan/Cambridge, U.K: William B. Eerdmans Publishing Company.

Marshall, Sherrin, ed. 1989. *Women in Reformation and Counter-Reformation*

Europe: Public and Private Words. Bloomington: Indiana University Press.

McGinn, Bernard. 1996. "The Changing Shape of Late Medieval Mysticism." *Church History* 65/2: 197-219.

McGrath, Alistair. 1999. *Spirituality*. Oxford: Blackwell Publishers.

McIntosh, Mark. 2000. *Mysteries of Faith*. Cambridge, Mass: Cowley Publications.

Peura, Simo. 1998. "Christ as Favor and Gift: The Challenge of Luther's Understanding of Justification." Pages 42-69 in *Union With Christ: The New Finnish Interpretation of Luther*. Edited by Carl E. Braaten and Robert W. Jenson. Grand Rapids, Michigan/Cambridge, U.K: William B. Eerdmans Publishing Company.

Peura, Simo. 2000. "The Essence of Luther's Spirituality." *Seminary Ridge Review* Winter 2000:16-33.

Raunio, Antti. 1993. *Die Summe des Christlichen Lebens. Die "Goldene Regel" als Gesetz der Liebe in der Theologie Martin Luthers von 1510 bis 1527*. Systemaattisen theologian laitoksen julkaisuja 13. Helsinki: Universitat Helsinki.

Roper, Lyndal. 1989. *The Holy Household: Women and Morals in Reformation Augsburg*. Oxford: Clarendon Press.

Treu, Martin. 1999. "Katharina von Bora, the Woman at Luther's Side." *Lutheran Quarterly* 13/2:157-178.

Wiesner-Hanks, Merry, ed. 1999. *Convents Confront the Reformation: Catholic and Protestant Nuns in Germany*. Marquette University Press: Milwaukee.

Liturgical Piety and Formation in Theological Education

Mark W. Oldenburg

The title of this piece may pretty well guarantee that it will not be read. The first two words in it will set off many alarms and close not a few minds. Even among those interested in spirituality, "piety" still leaves a bad flavor. And a goodly percentage of those who are left will see "liturgical," and hurry through to the next article. Since this article addresses a lively and important topic—how the practice and understanding of communal worship might shape public leaders of the church—I will be sorry if many skip it.

For the few who remain, let me begin with some definitions, which may explain why I use such a self-destructive title. "Piety" can mean either of two things. First, I often use the term to refer to an unexamined, pre-, sub-, and super-rational understanding of God and our life of faith. That is, if someone wakes you up at 3 a.m. and asks you what God is like, what you answer before you are fully conscious is a good clue to your piety. If a particular service, writing, picture, argument bothers you before you can explain why, that discomfort is reflective of your piety. Second, piety can also refer to the style of life which one's spirituality engenders. If there is a single relationship to which all of our life is connected and bound (my working definition of spirituality), then that relationship will color our attitudes and actions. We will pray in certain ways, meditate in certain ways, use our time, money, and abilities in certain ways, vote in certain ways, greet visitors in certain ways, refrain from certain words and actions. For some people, refusing to dance is an expression of their piety, since they see it as expressing or kindling an intimacy reserved for private, covenanted moments. For others, dancing is an expression of their piety, either because it expresses a joy which is appropriate for public occasions, or because it assumes a lack of self-consciousness which depends on the confidence of grace.

In general, however, piety is a living out of one's spirituality in the practice of one's life. It is akin to Luther's concept of *tentatio*—trial—in his reform of the *lectio divina*. Where the medieval practice of spiritual reading ended with contemplation and meditation, he stretched it to continue outside of the study, after the time of meditation had concluded. He urged practitioners to "test out" what they had heard in meditating on the psalms in the way they led the whole of their lives, and to see such testing out as an integral part of the spiritual discipline (LW 34:285-287).

And "liturgy" refers not to a formulaic, ritualized form of worship, but rather to worship which is, in the root meaning of the word, "the people's work." It is worship which is public and communal, where the whole congregation is, under God, the actor. The opposite of liturgical worship is not free or spontaneous worship, but worship where the leader is the central figure and the congregation is secondary, or even irrelevant. Thus, worship among Quakers and worship in the African-American tradition are among the most liturgical of services.

"Liturgical piety," therefore, is less a single type of devotional practice (saying the hours, for instance) than an approach to the disciplined Christian life which takes seriously the connections between the communal worship of the church and the experience, desires, and prayer life of the faithful. Each feeds, sustains, informs, depends upon, and complements the other.

For years I resisted requests to teach a course in devotional practice. The notion of students praying for credit, and of my grading their efforts seemed equally bizarre. But wise students helped me to realize that I was already teaching "liturgical piety" in the introductory course on worship, as well as in courses in hymnody, the church year, liturgical theology, occasional services, liturgical language. That is, I was spinning out the implications of communal worship for people's life of prayer and life in the world. I decided to offer a course, which I have offered occasionally since, in "The Practice of Liturgical Piety." And I decided to continue to include the consideration of liturgical piety in the rest of the courses I teach.

One way to explain this part of ministerial formation—offered in courses, retreats, and conversation—is to model it. I will take a single example from each of the four parts of the underlying shape of the Communion service in the West. Of course, this exercise will be far from exhaustive. There are many facets of each stage of the *ordo* to which I will attend. I will ignore occasional services entirely, although several books have already been written on how weddings help to undergird marriages, funerals help us to grieve and heal, and so on. Hymnody and the rhythms of the church year obviously serve as important sources for the nourishment of prayer life and lifestyle. But a single example each from Gathering, Word, Meal, and Sending may serve as examples for how Christians, and particularly the Church's public leaders, are shaped by their public worship.

Western Christians hold the *ordo* in common, as well as many of its specific texts. Our practices and understandings are not, however, identical. By conviction, as well as because of my promises at ordination and installation as a professor, I am bound to teach in accordance with the Lutheran confessions. These examples, then, will come from that perspective. They are intended to illustrate how liturgical piety is addressed in my work in theological education; they do not pretend to be universal or prescriptive.

Gathering—The Salutation

It is a short exchange—nine words in English, only six in Latin—which is easily overlooked. And yet it is a defining moment in the relationship between a community and its leaders. "The Lord be with you." "And also with you." It is a greeting older than the church. In Scripture it is found, among other places, in the books of Judges and Ruth. Most importantly, however, it is found in Luke: it is the way the angel Gabriel greeted Mary when she was offered the chance to bear Jesus. The leader looks the assembly in the eye and identifies them with Mary. "You," the greeting says, "are bearers of the Eternal Word. You are God's chosen instrument to inflesh the Son. If the Incarnation is to happen, it will happen with your cooperation, your pain, and your joy." Like Mary, all Christians, the greeting claims, are pregnant with the Son of God.

This greeting subverts all hierarchical arrogance. The leader looks at the assembly, and hails them with the titles of the Virgin—"Mother of God. Queen of Heaven. Higher than the cherubim. More glorious than the seraphim." And the assembly looks back and hails the leader in the same way, with the same respect. It is not the only time that happens in a service, of course. Also in the absolution, the sharing of the peace, the words of distribution, Christians give extravagant respect to people whose foibles, pettiness, sin and finitude they know all too well. That is one of the glories and scandals of a worshiping community—we are not safe in anonymity; we get to see as members of the body of Christ not only strangers we can idealize, but people we know. The recognition of others as beloved by God and the assurance of oneself being one beloved by God trumps our human divisions and divisiveness.

But respect is not all that Gabriel offered Mary at the Annunciation, nor all that the leader and the assembly offer each other in the salutation. Pregnancy is not a permanent state; it must be followed by birth. And so, being a bearer of the Eternal Word implies that one also is a deliverer of the Eternal Word. The salutation carries with it an expectation of witness, in word and deed. It is a reminder and call to action. Embedded in the salutation is the fundamental grammar of the Christian life—indicative followed by imperative; assurance followed by command.

The salutation is a text especially rich in meaning. But it is not unique. The liturgical texts spoken over and over, learned by heart, gotten under our skin are worth having there. We are formed (at least subliminally and, one hopes, consciously as well) by the words we speak. It is not only the obvious ones, like the creeds, which reward this sort of attention and contemplation. The *Agnus Dei*, for instance, does not only offer the assurance of Christ's effective sacrifice (in its transformation of the sacrificial system of Passover and *Yom Kippur*). Notice, too, that at its heart it is a pleading for the world: "you take away the sins of the world: have mercy on us, grant us peace." Here at the church's most intimate moment with Christ, it uses the term "us" not just for the household of faith, but for all humanity, all of the world, all of the cosmos. The familiar texts of our worship service, such as the salutation, are deep fountains of meaning—of consolation and challenge not only for the assembly, but even for its leaders.

Word—Writing the Sermon

One question I have never been able to answer is how much time I spend in sermon preparation. Especially as a parish pastor, I usually do not know when I am working on a sermon and when I am not. It is fairly easy to figure out how much time I spend on exegesis. But I find, when I get to writing out my outline, that the sermon draws on a hospital call here and a catechetics class there, a headline in Tuesday's paper and a conversation overheard on Thursday in the 7-11, this counseling session and that finance committee meeting.

Preachers are blessed by being forced to do what everyone would benefit from. Preachers have to immerse themselves in the lessons, and bring every tool to bear on understanding them in their own context. And they have to keep their eyes and ears open for echoes of those lessons in their context throughout the week. That familiarity with Scripture, and that attention to the ongoing work and will of God lie behind such classic, universal spiritual disciplines as *lectio divina* and the Ignatian exercises. And if preachers are too weak-willed to follow that discipline for its own sake and reward, we have Sunday's sermon hanging over our heads, an assignment which is due every week without the possibility of an extension!

The spiritual quest of many is for integrity—a deeper and more satisfying connection between all the parts of one's life. Preachers are forced to be on that quest constantly, especially those who live in, serve with, and preach in a single community week after week. We get to listen to the hopes and fears of the individuals and of the whole assembly, and to fit them into the story of God's constant wooing of humanity. As one of my professors said, in his Pennsylvania Dutch way, "Life for a preacher is like a pig for a butcher. You use everything."

Now, other tasks of leadership in the church are similarly blessed and integrative and daunting. Presiding, for instance, calls on many of the same gifts as preaching. Just as preachers need to know how humor and honesty, story and song work in their community, presiders needs to know how hospitality and order, prayer and praise work in theirs. The author of the prayers of the people gets to juggle the needs and dreams of the assembly with the promises and challenges of God in much the same way, and with much the same intimacy as the preacher. In many ways, the prayers of intercession are every bit as central to deacons as the sermon is to presbyters and bishops. And every part of a cantor's week leads up to enabling the congregation to sing together with insight and fervor and fidelity.

These weekly peak experiences of leadership of the community make it clear that public leadership in the church is not simply a job. Don't get me wrong—it is not where public leaders get our identity (preachers receive that in the font and from the pulpit, not in the pulpit!). But if we preach with honesty, there are no times when we can slough off that task. Even when we are not thinking about it, we are doing it. In bed with our spouse, on the diamond with the team, shoveling snow with the sexton—it is all sermon preparation. No place is safe!

Meal—the Incarnation as Paradigm

Luther's explanation of Christ's presence in the Supper, memorized by millions from the Small Catechism, is deceptively simple. Jesus' body and blood are present "in, with, and under" the elements of bread and wine. Within that simplicity, however, is the denial of two more popular explanations of the presence. As he did at greater length in "The Babylonian Captivity of the Church" (LW 36:3-126), Luther rejected the Roman Catholic doctrine of transubstantiation, which holds (in the language of Aristotelian categories) that the created nature of the elements needed to be done away with and replaced by the very substance of the body and blood of Christ. Further, as he did with greater fervor at the Marburg Colloquy (1529), Luther rejected Zwingli's doctrine of memorialism, which holds that Christ's body was located in heaven and was therefore unavailable on earth after the Ascension. Zwingli taught (and Calvin after him with considerably more nuanced and profound teaching) that the bread and wine are God-given *aides de mémoire*, allowing the believer's mind to focus on the promise of God. The sacraments, for the reformer of Zurich, were divinely appointed exceptions to the general rule that the material distracts the believer from the spiritual.

Lutheran rejection of transubstantiation and memorialism, reinforced not only in catechesis and preaching, but weekly in words of invitation and distribution, generate particular and peculiar pieties. Behind them both is the notion that the Incarnation is not an exception, but a general rule for God's communication. The affirmation that Jesus is fully human and fully divine is not simply a christological affirmation. It is the paradigm for God's way in wooing the world. God's Word (centrally Jesus Christ, but generally any self-revelation) normally comes through physical, ordinary, every-day means. It is no surprise that Israel's kings received their divine instructions not directly in visions, but through visiting prophets who said, "This is the Word of the Lord," often using audio-visual tools (figs, yokes, staffs, clothes, or the lack of them). God normally comes through the commonplace and material. The philosophical phrase for this understanding is *finitum capax infiniti*—the finite is capable of the infinite—which means that the creaturely can do more than simply remind us of God's Word, and do it without losing its character as creaturely.

This affirmation (and the dual rejections) indeed generates a peculiarly incarnational piety. The same impulse which rejects transubstantiation also rejects an assumed perfection in any vessel of God's Word. One does not have to choose, for instance, between studying the Bible as a human document and studying it as the Word of God. In fact, just as rejecting the humanity or divinity of Jesus leads eventually to misunderstanding both, one can only immerse oneself in one of those Biblical studies by immersing oneself in both. Likewise, one does not expect the church, the body of Christ, to escape being a sociological gathering and institution. It should not come as a surprise that family systems, tribal loyalties, patterns of leadership, and so forth, have an effect on the church. These are signs not just of sin or finitude, but incarnation; they might be destructive or inconvenient and are also on occasion constructive and useful, but they are inescapable, given God's way in the world. Seeing the bread and wine as bearing the body and blood of Christ, while remaining bread and wine allows for a certain measure of self-acceptance from all "bearers of the Eternal Word:" we need not stop being ourselves in order to bear the Gospel. Nor does this lead to stagnation and complacency; living in the process of being liberated from sin and death makes us more, not less, of ourselves.

On the other hand, the same impulse that rejects bare memorialism also rejects notions that the spiritual must be preserved from infection from the material. Rather, if the Incarnation is paradigmatic, God, who created both material and spiritual, constantly links the two together. Thus, for instance, in considering the church, structure and spirit are not of their nature incompatible. Constitutions, church buildings, institutions for relief or education, and guidelines about interpersonal boundaries are not *prima facie* betrayals of the mission and vision of the church, but ways of serving it. Of course, one can spend too much time and attention on them and they can even become idols or magical charms, but that is the chance God takes over and over again—with the institution of the *mezuzah*, and the commissioning of the twelve apostles and the six deacons, for instance.

More positively, the affirmation that the commonplace and earthly can indeed bear God's Word leads us to look for that bearing in our lives, and most especially in our relationships. It is through the love, patience, goading, and sacrifice of friends, parents, spouses, children, teachers, healers, guardians, and lovers that we understand with particular poignancy the God who delights in (and defines!) all these titles. Receiving Christ's benefits at the Table does not only lead us to look for them at all our other tables; it also leads us to look for them in all our relationships. This meditation—with thanksgiving as well as intercession—on our life's companions as icons and agents of God—is one of the most rewarding of spiritual disciplines.

This section has outlined a few of the pious implications of one understanding of the presence of Christ in the Eucharist. It is not meant to denigrate other understandings—even those which are rejected. These generate their own pieties, some of them identical, and others complementary to those outlined here. Both transubstantiation and memorialism, for instance, lend themselves better to pieties of personal and societal transformation than does the Lutheran understanding. But one of the many rewards of teaching in a denominational seminary is to shock students, who assume that their own tradition is vapid, with its fecundity.

Sending—The Dismissal

The very existence of this section of the *ordo* is surprising enough. The service carries within its very structure its own limitation. Faithful worship does not offer a haven, but of its nature impels worshipers to leave. The dynamic is that of the last stanza of the Gospel hymn, "In the Garden." The singer wishes to delight in intimacy with Christ, but realizes that the suffering of the world is itself the voice of God, calling her (the singer is obviously Mary Magdalene) out into service.

The short conversation between assisting minister and congregation which ends the Communion service in the *Lutheran Book of Worship* sums this up well: "Go in peace. Serve the Lord." "Thanks be to God." "Peace"—the gift given by the Resurrected Christ to his followers, claimed in the Kyrie litany at the beginning of the service, shared before the Table—is presupposed. Not only are the members of the assembly recipients of the peace of God, that peace is not limited to this gathering. Rather, the members take it with them as they leave.

And our service of God is not what we did in the last hour. In fact, what we did in the last hour is much more God's service of us. Now begins our true service in response. One of my favorite congregations has, over the doors leading out of the church, a sign which the worshipers only see as they leave the service to go out into the world. The sign says "Servants' Entrance." And this is not just duty, but most certainly delight. The invitation, even the command, to join God in service in the world is itself something to which we respond with joy and gratitude. The congregation's response is "Thanks be to God," not "Oh, all right."

One of my colleagues has often mused that, as often as

she's heard that conversation, it has been very rare that anyone has checked up on it. It is good and true that this bit of dialog implies that, living in the peace we receive, we see every moment of the next 167 hours as joining God in service in the world. But would it not be a good practice, she wondered, if people were to gather together sometime within that week, and let each other know how that is going. How has the peace been reinforced and challenged? How have opportunities for service presented themselves—at work and home, voting booth and bowling alley? What a fine expression of *koinonia*, to use this excuse to carry on mutual conversation and consolation!

Conclusion

Do the sorts of reflections just modeled belong in a seminary course in liturgics? They are a far cry from memorizing the genealogies and distinctive traits of the various German church orders of the 16th century. They are even a far cry from learning about the movements and gestures helpful for leaders of worship. But it would be unthinkable to teach worship without pointing out the relationships among the practice and leadership of communal worship, the understandings of God that they imply, and the implications of that practice and those understandings for all of life. Such reflections demonstrate the formative power of communal worship, as well as its devotional depth. And as I wanted to point out, it is by engendering piety—in the senses both of pre-conscious understandings of God and of lifestyle reflective of relationship with that God—that worship spiritually forms Christians, including public leaders in the church. And part of the piety of those leaders is, please God, a love for the assembly and its shared task.

Lament's Hope

Brooks Schramm

"Truly you are a God who hides yourself, O God of Israel, Savior." This passage from Isaiah is the source and inspiration of Luther's concept of *Deus absconditus*, the hidden God. *Deus absconditus* is in fact a direct quote from St. Jerome's Latin translation of Isa 45:15, which in turn directly influenced Luther's German rendering, *ein verborgener Gott*. As radical a notion as this is, it can be argued that the Hebrew text of Isa 45:15 is more radical yet. In the Hebrew text, God is not merely hidden (implying that God can perhaps be found if only one knows where or how to look) but rather God is one who actively hides. In other words, God does not just happen to be hidden but rather wills to be so. This hidden, or better, this hiding God is in the center of my own theology and piety, as I have been persuaded by the categorical claim of Gerhard von Rad: "All true knowledge of God begins with the knowledge of [God's] hiddenness" (von Rad 1965, 377).

Spirituality is a term defined and used in myriad ways. I use the term spirituality as another way of speaking of piety or the life of faith. It is impossible for me to think the topic of spirituality apart from the topic of prayer, and as an Old Testament teacher it is equally impossible to think prayer apart from the Psalter. This essay will focus on a particular type of psalm, namely, the lament psalm, and argue for its ongoing contemporary significance for the life of faith. No attempt is made here to corner the market, but rather to suggest lament itself as an indispensable aspect of a contemporary Christian (and Lutheran) spirituality and the lament psalm, therefore, as an indispensable resource for such spirituality. I make this claim because the lament psalm and lament itself guard spirituality against escapism, sentimentality, or simple optimism. Finally, it is argued that lamentation and the God who hides are inextricably linked.

Structure and Movement of Lament Psalms

The word lament is not commonly used in contemporary American English discourse. When it is used, it has an antiquarian ring and can suggest a range of meanings. When, however, Old Testament scholars use the term to refer to a particular type of psalm, lament has a specific, technical meaning. Lament means complaint. Lament psalms are complaint psalms. In a lament psalm, the psalmist is distressed and anguished about a state of affairs. But the key is that the psalmist is not resigned to the situation. The psalmist wants something to be done about it. Lamentation in the Psalter is, therefore, not about passive resignation but active complaining.

It is to be noted as well that lament psalms are not vaguely directed. They are all addressed specifically to God, to the one who, the psalmist believes, not only can but will do something about the situation. "For those who lament in the Old Testament, God is the One who can take away suffering" (Westermann 1994, 91).

Lament psalms, commonly divided into individual and communal laments, are the most common type of psalm, and they predominate overwhelmingly in the first half of the Psalter. The next most common psalm type is the thanksgiving or praise psalm, which predominates in the second half of the Psalter. On the one hand, the Psalter as a whole is structured, or moves, in the direction of praise and thanksgiving. But on the other hand, it is to be noted that praise or thanksgiving psalms are actually resolved laments and share all of the same presuppositions as the lament psalms themselves. Thanksgiving psalms are lament psalms "restated after the crisis has been dealt with" (Brueggemann 1995, 99). It is in this sense that praise and thanksgiving in the Psalter can be said to be dependent on lament. Thus, the Psalter as a whole is saturated with the language of lament, whether lament proper or lament resolved; in other words, with the language of complaint and the resolution of complaint. Without lament, and without the presuppositions inherent in lament, there would be no Psalter.

Lament psalms are tightly structured, that is, they are organized according to a standard and clearly recognizable pattern: invocation, complaint, supplication, vow of praise. They may vary in length, but the basic components are invariably there. The pattern, with slight variations, looks like this:

> God
> I/we have a problem
> Why have You allowed this to happen to me/us?
>> How long do I/we have to put up with this?
> I/we know that You can do something about it
>> You ought to do something about it, because
>>> (You and I/we have history together)
>>> (You promised me/us)
>>> (You will look bad if you don't)
>>> (You are my/our only recourse)
> When You have done something about it, I/we will praise You

All of the lament psalms (with the apparent exception of Ps 88) contain the striking assertion of trust in God to act in response, and thus end on something like a high note. The expression of trust is such a significant component that some scholars refer to lament psalms as trust psalms (psalms of trust). Much can be made of this structural characteristic, but two points are crucial. First, in the Psalter one does not lament for lament's sake. The one or ones lamenting expect (even demand) a change in the situation. Second, the lament psalm is a hopeful genre.[17] Sometimes petty, sometimes haunting, sometimes neuralgic, sometimes deeply troubling, lament psalms are united in the conviction that God will act in response.

Psalm 13 is an example of a typical lament psalm and illustrates many of the points made here:

For the leader. A psalm of David.
How long, O LORD; will You ignore me forever?
How long will You hide Your face from me?
How long will I have cares on my mind,
> Grief in my heart all day?
How long will my enemy have the upper hand?
Look at me, answer me, O LORD, my God!
Restore the luster to my eyes,
> lest I sleep the sleep of death;
> lest my enemy say, "I have overcome him,"
> my foes exult when I totter.
But I trust in Your faithfulness,
> my heart will exult in Your deliverance.
I will sing to the LORD,
> For He has been good to me.[18]

Given the virtual omnipresence of lament psalms in the Psalter, and given the hyperbolic words of reverential praise that Christians often utter about the Psalter, it is striking how absent lament psalms have been in formal Christian (especially Protestant) prayer.[19] To be sure, Christian prayer, particularly in the West, has had a fondness for the seven so-called penitential psalms (6; 32; 38; 51; 102; 130; 143). The penitential psalm is a sub-category of the lament psalm, one which contains a confession of sin or guilt on the part of the speaker. These psalms, and particularly Ps 51, have played a central role in Christian (Lutheran!) life and piety.[20] But there is an oddity here. As Claus Westermann has argued: "It is extremely odd that preference for these [penitential] Psalms has lasted for centuries without anyone having ever asked why, among such a large number of Psalms, there are in fact so few Psalms of repentance" (Westermann 1981, 274).

So, why are there so few psalms of repentance? A simple answer is that repentance or confession is an occasional but not necessary element in the lament psalm genre, which implies that lament psalms are normally about something else: lament psalms are more interested in suffering than they are in sin. Most lament psalms that do speak of sin are far more interested in the sins inflicted on the sufferer(s) than in sins committed by the sufferer(s). Most lament psalms either make no reference at all to sins committed by the sufferer(s), or they proclaim innocence, which is something especially shocking to Lutheran ears.[21] But so it is.

Christian (Lutheran) preference for the penitential psalms reveals a strong theological prejudice, and this prejudice is far from disinterested. The claim is that the only legitimate avenue of approach to God is via confession and repentance. True piety, true spirituality, is penitential through and through. The prejudice is so strong that it has enabled generation after generation either to misread, i.e., to read all lament psalms as if they were penitential psalms, or, for all practical purposes, ignore the overwhelming majority of lament psalms. This in turn has had no small impact on Christian (Lutheran) life and practice.

Spirituality and Reality

Historical Christian theological prejudice against lament psalms is generated to some extent by distaste for the religious chutzpah imbedded in the lament. This chutzpah comes to the fore when, as is characteristic of lament psalms, the one complaining raises an accusation against God.[22] Claus Westermann, who has done ground-breaking work on the Psalter, argues that biblical laments arise out of extreme situations, situations "where an individual, or a community, has been afflicted with such severe suffering that it can no longer be comprehended" (Westermann 1994, 92). For such sufferers it is incomprehensible that God could be implicated in their suffering, and this very incomprehensibility gives rise to the accusation against God in the form of questions: "Why, O God?" "How long, O God?" "How could you allow this to happen to me/us, O God?" Lament psalms are a far cry from a position which would argue: confess your sins and patiently bear your suffering without complaint. The distinction between these two positions is identical to that between Job and his friends.

The prejudice, or the concern, or the suspicion manifest in historical Christian thinking that lament is somehow impious is profoundly non-biblical. Quite the contrary, "[i]n the Bible lamentation has genuine integrity; in the Bible, lamentation reflects the very nature of human existence" (Westermann 1994, 89). And it is accusation against God that gives lament its edge and reveals a chief component of the covenant: Israel's claim on God. The religious chutzpah of the lament, together with its accompanying accusation, is that it "forces a confrontation with what is incomprehensible in the way God acts" (Westermann 1994, 93). It is precisely this confrontation that provides the context for the sufferer to address God in the most humanly honest of ways, and to do so in the conviction that the one addressed is the one who can and will relieve the suffering.

In this light the question arises: what kind of religious life is it, what kind of Christian life is it, in which lament and accusation against God are viewed as theologically and spiritually illegitimate?

> Where accusation against God is rejected as improper for the life of prayer, on grounds such as that it is irreverent to reproach God for anything, it necessarily follows that a whole aspect of reality—namely, all that which is too terrible to comprehend—is arbitrarily ruled out of one's relationship with God. When one speaks with God, one has to keep still about such matters. That, in turn, means one's speech with God must ignore a significant chunk of experienced reality.

> A consequence of rejecting the accusation against God is also that a person, in the face of terrible catastrophes in the private and public realms, denies God. One finds oneself no longer capable, at all, of praying to the God who allows such to happen. In the place of turning away from God like this, the Bible knows of another possibility: the one who no longer comprehends God and his action still holds firmly to him by holding the incomprehensible up to God (Westermann 1994, 93). [23]

Westermann's argument, essentially, is that the inevitable consequence of the absence of genuine lament from formal Christian prayer is a *de facto* severing of God from crucial aspects of experienced reality, and that this severing amounts to nothing less than a denial of God. Strong language indeed. We should be clear that Westermann is not dismissing penitential spirituality as such. He is, however, pointing out severe problems in a spirituality that is only penitential.

In a provocatively titled article, "The Costly Loss of Lament," Walter Brueggemann has picked up on Westermann's critique, although his concern is not directed at penitential spirituality. He, too, sees lament as indispensable for the life of faith and argues that a faith which is biblically founded not only permits but actually requires lament as part of prayer. For Brueggemann, the significance of such a faith

> is that it shifts the calculus and redresses the distribution of power between the two parties, so that the petitionary party is taken seriously and the God who is addressed is newly engaged in the crisis in a way that puts God at risk. As the lesser, petitionary party (the psalm speaker) is legitimated, so the unmitigated supremacy of the greater party (God) is questioned, and God is made available to the petitioner. The basis for the conclusion that the petitioner is taken seriously and legitimately granted power in the relation is that the speech of the petitioner is heard, valued, and transmitted as serious speech. . . . The lament form thus concerns a redistribution of power (Brueggemann 1995, 101-2).

Seen in this light, lament represents the stubborn insistence that something is wrong and God is, somehow, involved.

But what happens when lament is absent or ruled out of order? First, "genuine covenant interaction" is lost. When lament is not permitted, the voice of the petitioner is either silenced, or it is restricted to voicing only praise and thanksgiving to God. The result is a faith best characterized as a kind of "celebrative, consenting silence" that is at odds with reality. God can only be praised, not questioned, and God comes off like a king who surrounds himself only with dutiful "yes-men" and "yes-women" (Brueggemann 1995, 102).

The absence of lament involves a second loss as well: "the stifling of the question of theodicy" (Brueggemann 1995, 104). Theodicy is the traditional term given to attempts to justify the ways of God, that is, to exonerate God or to prove God's innocence vis-à-vis suffering and evil. Examples would be the claim that, when difficulties emerge, things are simply the way they are supposed to be, or that though things do not appear to be the way they ought to be, they really are; it is just that human beings cannot perceive it. Traditional theodicies heavily emphasize the providential goodness and righteous judgment of God. To be sure, lament psalms presuppose this as well, but they want to insist that there are glitches in the system, and that these glitches threaten to undermine the whole system. For Brueggemann, the loss of lament means that theodicy can never really be an open question, and, as a result, glitches in the system are simply denied.

Thus, one could say that what is at stake in lament is, finally, the dark side of reality. Is voice given in prayer to lived reality in its fullness, or is it stifled and swept under the rug in the name of a dignified or optimistic piety?

Israel's laments do not shy away from lived reality, for these laments are no strangers to the dark side of life. For people who live and who study theology in the wake of the unspeakable carnage that was the 20th century, confrontation with the dark side of life ought to be unavoidable. What kind of prayer would it be that can pray to God in the wake of the 20th century and not lament? Exhortations to "always look on the bright side of life" or empty platitudes about "God being good all the time" strike as something more than disingenuous, especially if one is willing to acknowledge, with Paul Ricoeur, "the terror of history." It was a quarter of a century ago that Irving Greenberg challenged teachers and students of theology with the significance of the lived reality that was Auschwitz: "No statement, theological or otherwise, should be made that would not be credible in the presence of the burning children" (cited in Linafelt 2000, 53).

What does it mean to pray to a God who rules over a world in which things like Auschwitz happen? What does it mean to pray to a God who rules over a world in which things like _____ happen? For teachers and students of theology in our day, these simply must be "front and center" questions. Such questions dare not be relegated to the margins. Lament refuses to let questions such as these go unsaid. Lament can be criticized, it can be stifled, it can be labeled impious or unspiritual, but lament only wants one thing: to hold lived reality up to God, to hold human suffering up to God. There is a basic human honesty about lament that qualifies as credible speech, and it is in this sense that lament helps to shape one's theological reflection and support one in practice.

The Hope of Lament

"Lamentation is the language of suffering" (Westermann 1994, 89). In lament psalms the voice of human suffering is heard, but the voice is not that of the primal scream, the inarticulate cry of pain or anguish. Lament psalms are written poems and thus stand at some remove from the primal moment. Deep feelings of suffering have been brought to coherent speech, and speech has in turn been raised to the level of poetry.

As the experience of suffering is poeticized, something happens to the descriptions of suffering: when one reads the laments it is difficult to pin down what exactly is going on, to know what exactly the nature of the suffering is. "Poetic language's tour de force is that it preserves enough concrete indications to keep the lament within the horizons of an individual experience and, thanks to a calculated indetermination, to raise the expression of suffering to the rank of a paradigm" (Ricoeur 1998, 215). Calculated indetermination or, what Ricoeur calls the "interplay of singularization and generalization," is a function of poetization and is what allows a poem (a psalm) to transcend its original, specific occasion and, thus, to be open for appropriation in other contexts.

But poetization does not only affect the description of the suffering. It also affects the identity of the one(s) who suffer(s). As Ricoeur puts it: "Words such as "I," "my," "you," and "your" lose their deictic function, which is to designate one particular individual. In this regard, one of the most extreme effects of the poetic style is to transform the "I" into an empty place capable of being occupied in each case anew by a different reader or auditor who, following the poet, can say: 'My God, my God'" (Ricoeur 1998, 215). It is through the poetization of suffering that lament psalms become available throughout the ages to those who suffer, and to those who pray on their behalf.

What does one get oneself into when praying a lament psalm? As stated earlier, in the Psalter one does not lament for lament's sake, rather lament is premised on the conviction that

God will hear and be moved to action. To pray the laments does not mean adopting a gloom and doom perspective, bitter pessimism, or a kind of stoic resignation. Lament is hopeful. Lament hopes in God. But what is the nature of this hope?

Patrick D. Miller has written: "Address to God in the Bible and in human life generally moves back and forth between plea or petition and praise or thanksgiving. In that movement, one is at the heart of what prayer is all about" (Miller 1994, 55). Similarly, Claus Westermann: "Praise of God gives voice to the joy of human existence; lamentation gives voice to sorrow. As the language of joy and the language of suffering, praise and lament belong together as expressions of human existence before God" (Westermann 1981, 11). These programmatic statements provide an avenue of approach to the question of the nature of lament's hope. Lament anticipates praise, and praise presupposes lament. Each is bound up with the other, and there is an oscillation between the two. Lament's hope emerges from the oscillation between these two interrelated phenomena.

Paul Ricoeur describes the hope being spoken of here as an "agonistic" hope, that is, a hope born of *agôn* (struggle). Such an understanding is significantly different from proposals that view the transition from lament to praise in terms of a straight-line, predictable, mechanical progression. For Ricoeur, the transition in lament psalms from lament to praise, from sorrow to joy, from the depths to the heights, is not an automatic transition but an agonistic one, first because the outcome of the struggle is never guaranteed. And second, praise and joy are not to be understood as the antitheses of lament and sorrow, rather lament and sorrow are taken up into praise and joy. Lament's hope, therefore, is a hope that emerges out of, or in the face of, real life, real struggle, and real human suffering. Perhaps this is not far removed from what Paul meant when he wrote: "And not only that, but we also boast in our sufferings, knowing that suffering produces endurance, and endurance produces character, and character produces hope" (Rom 5:3-4).

Conclusion

It is in lament that the experience of being abandoned, or forsaken, or ignored by God is given voice, and where the problem of *Deus absconditus*, the hidden God, emerges in its sharpest form. Lament as such does not attempt to justify suffering or derive meaning from it—it only wants God to relieve it or take it away. It wants God's compassion.

A contemporary spirituality informed and shaped by lament is one which is able to reckon with the tragic character of the human condition and which, nevertheless, finds a way to speak to God *aus tiefer Not*, out of the depths. In addition, one can say with Ricoeur that such a spirituality will be linked to "a personal and communal practice of compassion in regard to our human brothers and sisters who often are not so much guilty as suffering" (Ricoeur 1998, 232).

References

Brueggemann, Walter. 1995. "The Costly Loss of Lament." Pages 98-111 in Walter Brueggemann, *The Psalms and the Life of Faith*. Edited by Patrick D. Miller. Minneapolis: Fortress Press.

Linafelt, Tod. 2000. *Surviving Lamentations: Catastrophe, Lament, and Protest in the Afterlife of a Biblical Book*. Chicago and London: The University of Chicago Press.

Miller, Patrick D. 1994. *They Cried to the Lord: the Form and Theology of Biblical Prayer*. Minneapolis: Fortress Press.

Niebuhr, Richard R. 1969. "The Widened Heart." *Harvard Theological Review* 62/2:127-154.

Reu, M. 1934. *Luther's German Bible: An Historical Presentation Together with a Collection of Sources*. Columbus, Ohio: The Lutheran Book Concern.

Ricoeur, Paul. 1998. "Lamentation as Prayer." Pages 211-232 in André LaCocque and Paul Ricoeur, *Thinking Biblically: Exegetical and Herme-neutical Studies*. Translated by David Pellauer. Chicago and London: The University of Chicago Press.

Von Rad, Gerhard. 1965. *Old Testament Theology*, vol 2. Translated by D.M.G. Stalker. New York: Harper and Row, Publishers.

Westermann, Claus. 1981. *Praise and Lament in the Psalms*. Translated by Keith R. Crim and Richard N. Soulen. Atlanta: John Knox Press.

Westermann, Claus. 1990. *Die Klagelieder: Forschungsgeschichte und Auslegung*. Neukirchen-Vluyn: Neukirchener Verlag des Erziehungsvereins GmbH.

Westermann, Claus. 1994. *Lamentations: Issues and Interpretation*. Translated by Charles Muenchow. Minneapolis: Fortress Press.

Spirituality and Moral Action

Robin J. Steinke

The discipline of theological ethics and public life first gives attention to the multiple and varied ways that God is at work in the world and subsequently attends to the personal, corporate and institutional ways we respond to what God has already done in Christ through the power of the Holy Spirit.

The theme of this essay will endeavor to describe ways that spirituality is interwoven through the fabric of theological ethics and public life and will attend to the implications of spirituality for the church's mission in the world. I will approach spirituality as it is shaped through the gathered community at worship and as it is lived in the world, that is, *extra nos* (outside of one-self), rather than looking at the inner dimensions of spirituality or spirituality as a private, individual encounter with God. This chapter on spirituality is intentionally an outer directed project rather than an internal investigation of the mysteries of God's action within the human person. I will begin with attention to several theological definitions of spirituality. Subsequently, I will explore the way in which the community gathered for worship forms the community of believers spiritually and specifically empowers the community for responsible moral action in the world. Finally, I will briefly point to the implications of the grounding of this public face of spirituality through the church's *diakonia* or service with and for the world. This lays a theological foundation and demonstrates how spirituality with its focus *extra nos* calls for and invites this form of public theology in the world.

Multiple Meanings of Spirituality

The New Dictionary of Christian Ethics describes spirituality as encompassing "the whole of the lives of those who have responded to God's gracious call to live in fellowship with [him]" (Atkinson, et.al. 1995, 807-808). This would suggest that spirituality may be thought of as everything that we do and all of who we are. A gift of this perspective is that it mitigates against a compartmentalization of "spiritual" and "secular" dimensions of one's life. A challenge with this all encompassing definition of spirituality is that is seems to ignore or at least minimize the role of sin in persons and institutional structures. A definition of spirituality that has the self as the subject leans into the notion that spirituality is deepened through actions of the self. This would seem to deny the capacity of the self to "turn in upon itself." Any spirituality that is rooted within the self must take into account the capacity for self-delusion. When this self-delusion is taken to the institutional and structural level, spirituality that is inner directed fails to notice the impact of this self-delusion and its implications for the prevalence of systemic institutional evil.

Eugene Peterson, writing in a chapter called "The Seminary as a Place of Spiritual Formation" notes that "[s]pirituality, it seems, is not a function of place or curricula" (Peterson 1997, 56). He further illustrates the danger in instrumentalizing spirituality in the French phrase "deformation professionale," to refer to maladies that we are particularly liable to incur in the course of pursuing our line of work. Peterson notes that physicians risk becoming calloused to suffering and lawyers risk becoming calloused with respect to matters of justice. Those whose work is attending to the ministry of the Gospel risk becoming calloused to spiritual matters. Peterson moves us along in urging the necessity to pay attention to spirituality but stops short of a clear theological exposition of spirituality.

Wolfhart Pannenberg provides a clear point of departure in exploring the interconnectedness of spirituality and theological ethics and the implications for the public witness of the gospel.

He draws from Luther's idea of *extra nos* to make a case that spirituality is rooted in the larger life of God rather than in the self. Pannenberg writes that "whoever entrusts himself or herself, exists outside himself or herself, in the one in whom that person trusts. This is the famous *extra nos*, outside ourselves, that Luther so often emphasized" (Pannenberg 2001, 286). Participation in this new life in Christ, which trusts the promises of God who reconciled sinners to God's own self through the death and resurrection of Christ, is distinguished from a mysticism of humility. Pannenberg further notes that "participation in the new life of Christ and thus in God's own eternal life is to permeate our sense of Christian existence. That is Luther's contribution to our Christian spirituality" (Pannenberg 2001, 289). When one exists "outside of oneself" in faith, one participates in the righteousness of Christ. Participation in the righteousness of Christ means freedom from the ultimate power of sin and death and opens the way to restoration and renewal in Christ through the power of the Holy Spirit. This also implies that one has the freedom and vocation to respond to the call of the neighbor and to be invested in things beyond the sphere of self and one's own self-interest.

Rather than a person or community being consumed with self-preservation and self-interest, through this freedom in Christ persons are free to be open to the cries of the neighbor and indeed the world. Thus, in Pannenberg's interpretation of Luther, Luther's theology of justification serves as a basis for faithful action in the world, which is part of spiritual living.

Coherence of Spirituality and Worship

Spirituality, understood as something rooted outside of oneself in the faith of Christ which is given to one as a sinner who is justified, is nurtured and strengthened in a worshiping community. The worshiping community presupposes focus on the "other" rather than on the individual. Aspects of spirituality and worship are indeed personal, but theologically speaking, the focus and point of departure is the Triune God. Focus on this Godly model of self-giving in self-offering, and self-emptying provides a helpful corrective to being consumed with self-interest and self-absorption. Focus on spirituality which is outer-directed is not veiled language that does not honor the self, nor does it suggest self-abnegation as an appropriate way to honor God. This outer-directed spirituality in fact sees the self as beloved and as cherished by God.

This kind of spirituality, nurtured and strengthened in a worshiping community opens the way to God's work through the Holy Spirit to nurture a deeper relationship with the Triune God, with other persons and with the world. It is in this external focus, in this living *extra nos*, where spiritual flourishing "happens." And it is in this community, centered on God, shaped and nurtured by worship, and oriented toward the world, that one comes to know oneself better through the rich prism of the voice and presence of the holy other.

This has implications for those occasions when a person might not feel as though he or she is in the midst of God's work or living spiritually in one's daily life. There are times when a person might feel less than spiritual in his or her daily life as well as in worship. Spirituality which is based on the theological notion and impetus of *extra nos* is about living in obedience and response to God's action, where the litmus test of what is spiritual lies not in how it feels, subject to the whims of personal preference, mood, or the exigencies of circumstance, but in God's own self and the way in which a community is shaped through worship to be God's agents in the world.

Coherence of Worship and Ethics

The danger in arguing that spirituality in the form of worship shapes persons and communities for responsible moral action in the world is the risk of instrumentalizing worship. Worship can become a means to an end rather an end in itself. The primary focus of worship is on the Triune God. God is the focus in that God speaks a word of address to the gathered community through the absolution, in the reading of the word and the preaching of the gospel. God is the one to whom praise and prayers are addressed. The focus is not on what techniques can be employed to produce a deeper spirituality and responsible moral agents for the world. Any attempt to "commodify" worship risks distraction from the one who calls, enlightens and sanctifies the gathered community, the Triune God.

Hans Ulrich writes that "the worshiping community, the communion of saints, as the place where the Word is heard, is inalterably bound up with the foundations of ethics" (Bayer and Suggate, 1996, 29). The faith community gathered in worship is the constitutive place where the Christian learns to live ethically and grows in Christian character. To be "led by the Spirit" (Rom 8:14) and to "live by and be guided by the Spirit" (Gal 5:25) means that one begins not first asking what one should do in this or that ethical situation. Rather, one begins with the gathered community of faith around Word and the baptismal water, confession and forgiveness, bread and wine, law and gospel. If spirituality describes the life of the Christian in relationship to the Triune God who creates the world, claims all sinners in the faith of Christ and sustains persons for the responsible life of faith in community, then the community gathered in worship provides an appropriate place to think about how corporate spirituality makes moral claims on persons.

Spirituality devoid of an external focus has the danger of self-absorption, self-interest and self-serving. Rooting responsible moral action in worship relocates the center of attention from the self to the holy other. Being grafted into the larger life of God changes one's own wants and desires to God's desires for the world. This means that Spirituality can be described and understood as conformity to the life of Christ (1 Cor 12).

In the worshiping community where one is shaped by the cross of Christ and receives the invitation to serve the neighbor, where one's deepest longings and desires change over time, and where the focus shifts from the self to God, one cannot help but become more attuned to the needs of the neighbor. One starts to see the neighbor through the eyes of Christ. In fact, an expansion takes place in who one understands the neighbor to be, because one is grafted into the larger life of God and is changed so as to see the other with the love and compassion of Christ.

It eventually becomes insufficient simply to pray for the poor or the lonely, because one is drawn into the lives of those for whom prayer is offered through direct action and service. This action takes many forms including perhaps staffing a soup kitchen or food pantry or becoming involved in advocacy and attending to systemic causes of poverty.

I want to employ the *ordo* used in worship as a framework for thinking about the moral demands of spirituality. The gathering, word, meal and sending in the liturgy provide entry points for seeing clearly the links between spirituality and moral action and how that action is nurtured. This framework functions much like chord progressions in a jazz piece. The improvisations on the theme are nearly infinite, but the structure provides a crucial framework so that one need not worry about what comes next but can enjoy the freedom which the structure provides.

Gathering Rite

The gathering rite begins at the font with a call to remember what God has done in us, through the Holy Spirit at baptism. This call to remembrance opens the way for the freedom to confess how we have failed in our responsibilities to God, to oneself and to the world. Hospitality is exercised in the form of invitation to all who are sinners, the freedom and possibility to confess and receive God's forgiveness. In the gathering rite a tone is set for spirituality that arises out of God's action in response to the utter poverty of one's creatureliness. As sinners, we cannot move toward God. God acts first to embrace us in all the fragilities, frailties and vulnerabilities we carry. Spirituality, expressed in worship, beginning in the gathering, is total trust in God's promises and reliance on the extravagance of God's goodness.

The Word

Moral action which draws from the well of spirituality rooted in the Word of God necessitates listening. Scripture is the point of departure for listening to the stories of God's work in the world. The Word of God informs how we understand our context, purpose and action. We sit in silence, not a vacuous silence but silence under the Word of God, to hear God's address to us. We listen to the grand narratives of God's promises and hear how our lives are touched by God's gracious action.

Listening to the Word requires patience and time. In an age of instant access, instant response, instant food, instant messaging, the notion that spirituality, drawn deeply from the well of attentive listening to the Word of God over long periods of time, seems anathema to our post-modern ways of being in the world.

Listening to the Word of God is risky business. It requires openness and a vulnerability to be changed by the hearing of the Word in the encounter with the other. The possibility for change and transformation exists when listening actively in obedience to the Word of God.

Listening to the Word nurtures spirituality that is inspired and directed by God's Word and action for the world and in the world. The Gospel, as the Word which speaks in and for the world, is revealed in the most unlikely and unexpected places in the world. The church's call to *diakonia*, to service, is a call to be present in these unlikely places and witness to the ways that God is already at work. This kind of spirituality, rooted in God's Word, enters places of hurting, of poverty, of injustice, not out of arrogance or superiority that one has something to bring, but with the humility that this is a holy place because Christ has gone ahead of us and is in the midst of this suffering.

The Meal

All who gather around the table to share in the body and blood of Christ are in equal need of this life sustaining meal. Illusions about being "well off" are disabused in the words "this is the body of Christ, broken for you." Sam Wells, Vicar in an Anglican Parish in Cambridge, England, in writing about the virtues that are deepened through worship notes that in the Eucharist "[t]hey [Christians] are shaped in the virtue of hope, as they are given a picture of what the heavenly banquet will look like . . . They perceive that at the heart of fellowship is sacrifice" (Wells 2002, 73). Sharing the Eucharistic feast sustains persons for moral action in the world. The meal fosters spirituality that leads to concrete encounter with and service for the other.

The Sending

It is in the sending that we see the liturgical act and impetus for responsible moral action in the world. The assisting minister sends members of the congregation to their places of ministry in the world. Persons are sent to home, work, school, the unemployment line, the homeless shelter, the playground, anywhere that their vocation or circumstances take them, in order to testify through what they do and who they are that God reigns. In the spirituality of the sending, when God's agents for the world go out, it is to testify that suffering, poverty, disease, struggle, and death will not have the last word, for God has another ending in mind which is glimpsed at the Eucharistic feast, an ending in which God will triumph over the ultimate power of destruction and death, an ending where all will be fed and none will suffer.

The ecclesial dimension of this sending is the church's commitment to *diakonia*. Individuals are not only shaped for responsible moral action in the world but out of the life of the Triune God the church, as institution, also has a public responsibility to attend to the cries of the world. The Lutheran World Federation 2002 International Consultation on *diakonia* included the following statement in the Epistle to member churches:

> We are shaped to serve others through worship, where we celebrate God's gifts of grace in the Word, in water, in bread and wine, and glimpse the fulfillment of God's promise. In this broken world where sin and injustice abound, God in Christ through the power of the Holy Spirit shapes us as a gathered community. Thus, we become agents of grace, hands and feet of Christ for the healing of the world.

There are multiple levels of this kind of *diakonia* including, personal, congregational, churchwide and international. The churchwide and international expressions of *diakonia* include all social ministry organizations, healthcare institutions, advocacy organizations, educational institutions and the work of the Lutheran World Federation through its development agencies. These institutional expressions of *diakonia* animate the church's public face of spirituality. These are the vital organizations where we witness with and for the world on matters of hope, poverty, violence, health, peace and justice.

Social justice is constitutive of spirituality. Spirituality is marked not so much by a deeper discovery of oneself, but by a deeper recognition and response to others, both within the Christian community and perhaps especially those outside the Christian community. This kind of spirituality, living *extra nos*, outside of oneself and for the Triune God, for the neighbor and for the world, risks everything by trusting in God's promises of redemption, restoration and renewal. This risk has to do with daring to proceed with hope where despair looms. It has to do with encountering the world as it is and daring to trust that God is at work and will have the last say. It has to do with encountering neighbors as they are and in humility seeking to learn from the neighbor, even when they seem so different from oneself.

The chord progressions in jazz provide enormous possibilities for improvisation, for creativity and for beauty. The kind of spirituality to which I have pointed is not prescriptive, but like jazz improvisation, provides possibilities for theological imagination and gives perspective for creative engagement with the world in a manner faithful to God's promises for the world. This kind of spirituality, with the Triune God as its starting point and focused and oriented towards the world is at the heart of a Lutheran ethic.

References

Atkinson, David and David H. Field, eds. 1995. *New Dictionary of Christian Ethics and Pastoral Theology.* Leicester, England: Inter Varsity Press.

Bayer, Oswald and Alan Suggate. 1996. *Worship and Ethics: Lutherans and Anglicans in Dialogue.* New York: Walter de Gruyter.

Braaten, Carl E. 1974. *Eschatology and Ethics: Essays on the Theology and Ethics of the Kingdom of God.* Minneapolis: Augsburg.

Pannenberg, Wolfhart. 2001. "Luther's Contribution to Christian Spirituality." *Dialog* 40/4: 284-289.

Peterson, Eugene. 1997. *Subversive Spirituality.* Grand Rapids: Eerdmans.

Strohl, Jane. 2001. "Religion vs. Spirituality." *Dialog* 40/4:274-276.

Suggate, Alan. 2002. "Worship and Ethics: Reflections on Conversations Between Anglicans and Lutherans." *Studies in Christian Ethics* 15/1:54-65.

Welch, Sharon D. 1999. *Sweet Dreams in America: Making Ethics and Spirituality Work.* New York: Routledge.

Wells, Samuel. 2002. "How Common Worship Forms Local Character." *Studies in Christian Ethics* 15/1:66-74.

Space and Spirituality

Gerald Christianson

"We shape our buildings,
and afterwards our buildings shape us."
Winston Churchill

Apart from the spoken Word, the hymnbook and *Cat-echism* have probably contributed more to Christian formation than official denominational theology or knowledge of traditional history. Yet, even before we held our first hymnbook, or someone put a *Catechism* into our hands, we had already formed or been formed by a spirituality. Many historians of religion, as well as astute and gentle spirits like my venerated colleague and friend, Bengt Hoffman, think that this experience is grounded in a precognitive and often inarticulate sense of the holy (Hoffman 2003).

When Ray Foy, a Lutheran pastor in eastern Pennsylvania, prepared his Doctor of Ministry project some years ago, he developed a rigorous survey to determine his congregation's attitudes toward the Lord's Supper. One result was not surprising. In their more or less cognitive sacramental theology, members were more Zwinglian than Lutheran. Three other conclusions, however, caught my attention. Worshippers experienced the Eucharist as a re-enactment of the Last Supper. Consequently they held their minister in high esteem not because of the Office of Word and Sacrament, but because this person played the role of Jesus in the drama. Even more intriguing, the congregation felt a sense of mystery and inspiration during communion, not so much because they believed that Christ was present in the meal, but more because the place where they knelt—the chancel between the rail and the altar against the wall—was a holy place (Foy 1979). Mircea Eliade, the great historian of sacred spaces, would nod with approval (Eliade 1959).

Beyond the always fascinating study of the universal human tendency to be religious—singled out by Karl Barth and Dietrich Bonhoffer early in the last century as an enemy of the Gospel—our focus here is the specific shapes that our spirituality takes from our experience in and of a worship space. As a church historian interested in art and architecture, I also want to stress that these specific shapes of our spirituality arise early and formatively; that they continue powerfully to influence how we think about God and the Christian community; and that they are often taken for granted without reflection. To paraphrase Winston Churchill, we shape our worship spaces, and afterwards our worship spaces shape us.

Yet, despite the importance, even the fundamental nature, of the connection between space and spirituality, the subject has elicited little attention. Although the liturgical movement, reflecting the growth of modern biblical studies, has advocated the necessity of renewing worship forms since the beginning of the twentieth century (Senn 1997, 632-667), few theologians or liturgical scholars drew out the logic for church buildings and worship spaces.

Two practicing architects did. *Worship and Architecture*, Peter Hammond's pioneering essay of 1960, set an agenda of liturgical-architectural priorities that are valid today, but ironically Protestant churches were engaged in a building boom during the 1950's and 1960's, and advocates of the A-frame craze paid little heed. Although more accessible to American readers, *Architecture for Worship* (1973) by Lutheran architect Edward A. Sovik may have felt like a cold shower to those accustomed to traditional structures, and his call for a clean sweep may have seemed to go too far to be taken seriously. Sovik advocated a "secularization" of the church building and especially the sanctuary which he called "the Centrum." In place of standard two-volume interiors, a dark container for God and clergy, and a larger, lighter one for the rest, he wanted a congregational space around the altar-table that was no more than eight to ten rows removed from the liturgical action. A processional cross brought into this congregational space would say clearly that God is found in the midst of the community and not isolated in a chancel or out beyond the east wall.

Liturgical scholarship, however, no longer lags behind, and has recently produced a first-rate textbook, *Re-pitching the Tent* by Richard Giles (1999), written in part from the perspective that space is potentially formative. This study has also elicited the endorsement of the distinguished Protestant liturgical scholar, James White. Addressing the curricula of theological schools in 2001, White noted that seminaries "are at last facing up to the significant role that worship spaces play in the lives of their respective communities," and added,

> "I am quite willing to say that during a student's years in seminary the seminary chapel building will probably teach more about spirituality than any single faculty member" (White 2001, 103).

Noting "a contradiction of a servant ministry and a 'built ecclesiology' which we would hesitate to teach in the classroom but flaunt heedlessly in the chapel," White concluded that "buildings raise some fundamental theological questions about the nature of God and the church" (White 2001, 104).

In addition to contributions by scholars such as White, the study of how worship spaces shape our spirituality can be enhanced by recent biblical and historical research, the encouragement of enlightened denominational departments of architecture and worship that have assimilated the liturgical renewal movement, and the no less important insights of ordinary Christians. Charles Grube, for instance, has just completed a study of how he and his congregational leadership intentionally designed a new worship space to shape both the worshipers' perceptions and their habits (Grube 2004).

Although neither an architect nor a liturgical scholar, I first wrote on this subject over twenty years ago (Christianson 1982), but my curiosity in the dynamic relationship between space and spirituality was not prompted—at least not at the beginning—by expertise or academic interests. It was stimulated by a fire and an aging organ during a frenetic period in the early 1970's. Both fire and aging organ led to major revisions in worship spaces and both had considerable impact on their respective communities. And because they did, they can connect us to a broader spectrum of congregational experiences, and have more than passing relevance to our theme (See DeSanctis 2002).

The fire I refer to gutted the interior of St. James Church in downtown Gettysburg in January, 1969. In the months that followed it seemed mildly ironic that most conversations and occasional conflicts focused on the question of remaining in the same location, and on the arrangements for the Sunday School area. When the time came to decide on the "sanctuary," we on the worship committee approached our date with destiny with fear and trembling, but no serious objections were raised. The proposal sailed through without a dissenting vote even though it envisioned a dramatic, even radical, reorientation of the worship space.

Perhaps recent history had come to our aid. The Sunday School Movement remained strong at St. James, along with its independent worship "exercises," orchestra, hymnals, offerings and budget—not to mention its dedicated lay leadership and mildly anti-clerical sentiment—so that many members had a personal, proprietary investment in the Sunday School "auditorium," and allowed others to deal with the "clergy stuff." At the same time, however, we had prepared the ground for the changes in the worship area by formulating a brief and clear set of working principles that we shared and discussed with architects and congregation. When the members returned to their church home on a Sunday in May, 1971, they found that the whole enclosure had been reoriented from the far end of a long, rectangular space with an altar located in the chancel, to a gathering around a raised, but un-railed table on the long wall. The entire space was flexible, and all the furniture freestanding,.

We still lack an extensive body of precise studies on how such changes in worship spaces affect the spirituality of individuals or congregations, so that much of what was rewarding about the process at St. James remains anecdotal. To the extent that anecdote in this area of spirituality can serve as evidence, however, one could sense that the renewed interior allowed a new worship atmosphere. This was already evident at the opening service when members created a buzz of excitement over the new arrangement, seated around three sides of the table, and again when they greeted one another with the Peace. The Building Committee chair was certain that several members faced and spoke to one another in those early days whom they had seen for years but never known.

The second project involved the Gettysburg Seminary chapel—well before James White issued his appeal to seminary faculties and boards. Early in the tenure of President Herman G. Stuempfle, Jr., the original organ showed signs of aging. When the project was finally finished in the summer of 1980, not only was a new tracker organ installed on the east wall of the building, but the entire chancel, except the pulpit, had been cleared of fixed furniture, including the altar, choir pews, and chancel barrier. This allowed the congregation—in this case the student body, staff, and faculty—to gather around a substantial table set in the midst of the newly freed-up space.

None of this was done without considerable discussion, but the main issue focused more on the placement of the tracker organ than the replacement of the altar by a table. Since the liturgical movement had been introduced to the Seminary and began to flourish during the presidency of Donald R. Heiges in the mid 1960's, the community was frequently accustomed to gather around a small table placed in the narrow space between the choir pews on either side of the chancel. While again one cannot prove connections to faith or action—if these can be measured under any circumstances—it did appear more than coincidental that many graduates who had now experienced both celebration and closeness began to expand the worship horizons of their congregations with a greater emphasis on community, as well as more frequent parish communions.

A by-product of the experiences at St. James and the Seminary had the unintended effect of prompting my curiosity about a long-time scholarly suspicion: buildings say something to us as well as about us. Subsequently I began more or less systematically to incorporate reflections on the impact of space on spirituality in regular offerings of courses on "Christian Art and Spirituality." It is not the course, but the spirituality that concerns us here, and my purpose is to propose a two-part thesis about the intimate relationship between spirituality, architecture, and liturgy.

First, we take as self-evident the principle that buildings say something about us. For me, and for students who call it "art in the dark," it is one of the more interesting and enlightening ways to survey the broad course of church history and bring out the peculiar ethos of its succeeding chronological periods, whether early, Byzantine, or medieval; Renaissance, Reformation, or Baroque; Victorian, modern, or "post modern." In order to make this kind of analysis work, we assume the validity of what Sir John Summerson called the "Act of Settlement" that buildings were "right" for their time and place, and that they arose subconsciously from the hopes and aspirations of the people who built them. With this assumption we begin to differentiate styles and delineate differences, and in addition attempt to suggest something of the "mentality" (to use the French historical term) that characterized their age (Summerson 1970).

To illustrate with one random example (it was not in my *Michelen Guide*), I recently visited Portland, Maine—like so many New England seaboard towns, a historical seaport and early industrial center. I found myself one day in front of a monumental, Neo-Romanesque church edifice, and assumed that I was looking at an Episcopal or Roman Catholic church, but was taken back when I read that it was United Church of Christ (formerly Congregational). Where was the classic look of the New England meeting house that so many Americans admire and that seems to speak of simple, apostolic Christianity and open democracy?

With Summerson's "Act of Settlement" in mind, we can surmise that, somewhere during the late nineteenth or early twentieth century, this congregation began to rethink its roots and its role in American society, just as did many Lutheran, Episcopal, Catholic and even Congregational churches in this pluralistic society. No longer content with what now seemed primitive buildings housing innocuous worship services, and concerned that Christianity should not be too easily identified with contemporary culture, these churches began to seek a distinct identity that would reflect the long span of Christian tradition, especially the Middle Ages. Following such trendsetters as Trinity Church in Boston where Phillips Brooks was pastor, and Henry Hobson Richardson the architect, these American Protestants looked back beyond colonial history to what they conceived to be the beginnings of Europe, and thus demonstrate to themselves and their communities that their roots ran deep.

Ironically, when one enters these churches, including Portland, the interiors were often still thoroughgoing Protestant preaching spaces. No "popish vistas" here, thank you, although other Episcopal and Lutheran churches were happy to adopt the principles of the Oxford movement with chancels long enough to include divided choir stalls and high altars at the far end behind an altar rail. It was exactly this spirituality that had prompted our forebears at Gettysburg Seminary to build its magnificent chapel in the early 1940's and incorporate an Oxford Movement chancel within a fresh, but gracefully proportioned, copy of a colonial church.

Suffice to say that the first half of our proposition, that buildings say something about us, is a useful tool as well as a common way by which, consciously or not, we see our world and its churches. The second half of our proposition, that worship spaces say something to us, is of even greater interest, and far more profound for our study of spirituality, but not as readily grasped or appreciated. I have not forgotten that the worshippers in the very small and now defunct parish I served many years ago in Gary, Indiana, faced a simple, railed-off altar on the east wall. Whether intended or not, this orientation was prone to say, "God is up there." When we opened the gate that joined the two sides of the communion rail, we were affirming that "God is in this holy of holies, and only clergy (and male acolytes in those days) are welcome." And when the Words of Institution were said in this chancel while facing the altar without a full Eucharistic prayer, I was hinting that the minister brings God down through the repetition of a religious formula, even though I would have denied this proposition in preaching and conversation.

Since we are describing observed phenomena here, the approach we have adopted is called phenomenological. To put it another way, a Martian who observed us earthlings in this little gathering in Gary—or Portland or Gettysburg, for that matter—could easily perceive and depict the locus of God in these places, and the congregation's spirituality as a consequence. In Gary the piety was individualistic and stressed a one-to-one relationship with God that favored private meditation and silent prayer. If our Martian knew something about church history, he could ponder the similarities to the spirituality of the late medieval Mass with its concentration on the priest's action during the canon, and the consequent role of the congregation as devout spectators who, except at the moment of consecration, often spent their time devoutly saying their rosaries. All of these expressions of spirituality—Protestant and Catholic; medieval and modern—are profound, deeply felt, and have their own rationale, but they are remarkably similar despite what we may claim in our official theologies. They underline the point that architectural forms inform and buildings shape, not only the corporate liturgy but also the personal spirituality of the worshipers.

My colleague Nelson Strobert reminds us that, according to learning theory, we sometimes take action when we have been informed about something new, but that we also take action when something happens to us without formal cognitive instruction. A dramatic, and historic, example is Rosa Park's decision to sit at the front of a bus in Montgomery, Alabama. Americans had talked for a century about defeating Jim Crow, but this one action snowballed and confronted us with the need to accept new ways of living together. The impact of worship spaces on our spirituality works in a similar fashion. Before we are even informed about it or can give articulate expression to it we are shaped by it.

How space has actually shaped Christian spirituality over the long and varied course of church history and its manifestation in church buildings might seem a daunting subject until we notice that all churches fall into one of two categories. Scholars call these basic types *domus ecclesiae*, the house of the people of God manifested in the house church, and *domus dei*, the house of God manifested in the basilica. We can illustrate these types if we turn our attention to the contrast between their manifestations in the course of the early church.

After a century of modern biblical studies and liturgical renewal we are in a much better position to consider how these two disciplines have informed one another and especially how both have appropriated the understanding of *ecclesia* as the people of God, and *leiturgia* as the work of the people of God (Fenwick and Spinks 1995). Furthermore, we are in a better position to understand the significant function of the house church in the New Testament and the early Christian era, especially in the writings of Paul.

Early communities frequently gathered in homes, many of them owned by wealthy patrons, often women. Although some degree of privilege was probably accorded to these persons of wealth, the communities who gathered in their homes were open, with little or no hierarchy, both in the ecclesiastical sense and probably also in regard to gender. Whatever the status of their "ordination," we are certain that women played an important role, and led the way for what we would call social service, the remarkable program of support given to widows and orphans that attracted the attention of non-Christians. In worship, the community gathered at least every week for the sharing of Word and sacrament. The house where they met was simply that, a house, and had no particular religious character except for the words and actions of the community. The meal itself was simple, utilitarian, and domestic, befitting its setting in a home (Banks 1980).

The long-standing tradition that early Christians worshipped in the catacombs is only partially true. Cemeteries, including catacombs, were sometimes the site of memorial feasts on or near the grave of a loved one or a venerated martyr, but they were not a place for the weekly worship of the community. What is more curious is why the early church universally rejected pagan temples as appropriate places for their assemblies. One or two, including the magnificent Pantheon in Rome, were later converted for Christian use, but these were exceptions, perhaps meant to symbolize the Christian triumph over paganism. In any case, Christians did not turn their backs on temples simply because of their pagan associations. They had few qualms about converting the Roman date for the winter solstice, celebrating the birth of the unconquered sun, into the time for the festival of the Nativity, or adopting other useful, non-biblical practices.

The reason Christians rejected the temples reveals something profound about their spirituality and its visible forms. Pagan sanctuaries were largely exteriors. Even when seen today, structures such as the Parthenon in Athens, or the Greco-Roman temple in Nimes, known as the *Maison carré*, are serene, precise, logical, and balanced. Liturgically, the key element was the spacious portico in front of the building, as it had been in the sprawling Egyptian temples that preceded them. It was here that worshipers could gather for ceremonial sacrifices. Only the priests could enter the interior which, to the casual tourist today appears uninteresting and even sterile, especially in the absence of the statues which once adorned them.

In distinction to these buildings that emphasized their exteriors, early Christians wanted to go inside. They needed space for intimate, audible proclamation and a corporate, visible meal. Christians, in short, wanted secure inner spaces. Even as late as the astonishing Church of St. Vitalis in Ravenna, one finds little on the exterior to entice the visitor, except its unusual octagonal shape. The glory of the building, and of early Christian art, is the interior Eucharistic space enshrined in brilliant mosaics (Norberg-Schulz 1975, chaps. 3-4).

Given what building forms the early Christians rejected, it is not difficult to surmise what they preferred. We know from several sources, including Paul's memorable visit to Troas where he spoke so long that a sleepy listener fell out of the window, that early Christians gathered in upper rooms, often above merchant shops on the first floor. In such a room the apostles met with their Lord on the night he was betrayed. In addition, while the phrase "the church in the house of" could mean the extended family in this home, it also implied the building that patrons such as Lydia, Phoebe, and Priscilla opened to early communities for worship. Such references have prompted considerable speculation about what room in a Roman-style villa they might have gathered for Eucharist.

Most likely, it had to be a closed room, so the open courtyard at the center of a villa known as the atrium, was not likely the space Christians sought. That they preferred the living or dining room is what one would expect for a family that gathered to share a meal. This assumption was confirmed by the discovery during World War I of a little building in Dura Europus, a Roman garrison town on an isolated stretch of the Euphrates River in modern Syria. Dura shows that the Romans and their client populations were a very religious people, as Paul observed in Athens. Under the rubble along Dura's outer wall archeologists discovered several temples, among them structures dedicated to Bel and the Christians' chief rival, Mithra (now at Yale University), as well as a handsomely decorated synagogue.

Among these discoveries was a comparatively simple villa with rooms surrounding a central atrium. What makes this building more than an ordinary house is that the room off to one side has been transformed into a baptistery (also at Yale), and another room off to the other side enlarged by the removal of a wall, probably to accommodate the celebration of a meal. Recent discoveries near the graveyard under St. Peters in Rome lead us to surmise that house churches, or church-houses, were known in the capital as well. I remember walking down through the centuries, as it were, underneath St. Clement in Rome until we reached the corner of a Roman street where what appeared to be a Christian meeting house stood across from a Mithraum.

The house church at Dura and the accumulative archeological and literary evidence from the period before Constantine show that the earliest type of Christian building was a *domus ecclesiae*, an ordinary home that, when occasion demanded, provided a place for doing liturgy. Not only is *domus ecclesiae* a type of church building, it is a fundamental form of Christian spirituality.

Is it only the ravages of time that hide other house churches from our view? More likely it was the wide-spread, and in the West almost universal, adoption of the basilica, the concrete manifestation of the second type of church building, the *domus dei*.

The name basilica derives from the Greek term for "royal," and its prominence in the history of the Christian church is associated with a truly royal emperor, Constantine, to whose court we owe so much medieval ceremonial—from bowed heads and pointed hands to genuflections and clerical dress. Long before Constantine the Romans used basilicas for baths, market places, audience halls, and courts of justice. The irony is that Christians, having rejected pagan temples, accepted the buildings in which so many fellow Christians had received the death sentence. But adopt them they did, and in astonishing numbers.

These generally rectangular buildings proved exceedingly popular because they were so well adapted to the needs of post-Constantinian worship. They were usually commodious enough to accommodate large crowds, and still provided a simple space for the clergy in the apse—the semi-circular area jutting out at the east end which was once occupied by a royal personage or his image. Even so, the congregation still moved from the preaching platform to gather around the table for communion. Such was the staying power of the *domus ecclesiae* and its spirituality that Christians continued to use the early basilica as a modified house for the people of God.

Nevertheless, the classical basilica soon began to show a substantial shift toward a different type of spirituality. Some adaptation was necessary to accommodate the enormous influx of new members and the cult of martyrs in the post-Constantinian era. Consequently, the table was removed to the apse and the presiding minister and assistants took seats on the side. Now the people faced front, toward the apse, rather than gathered around the table. By the early Middle Ages the table had become an altar, enclosed to hold a martyr's relics, and further separated from the people by a rail.

This change accompanied a number of significant developments. Once the cup and bread were offered apart from a full meal, the necessity for a domestic setting was lessened. The community could now celebrate this streamlined supper in an assembly hall rather than a dining room. Formal seating arrangements and spatial differentiation arose. Clergy and laity became distinct, not by function as before, but by place. The presiding minister emerged as a cultic leader who was seen as a priest and who mediated God to the assembly. Even Eusebius, the first church historian and biographer of Constantine, did not scruple to compare churches to Solomon's temple (Branick 1989, 133).

Eventually theologians articulated what worshippers already experienced. In addition to serving as a rationale for appropriating elements of the Old Testament cult and its priest-hood, the widespread adoption of the basilica had given shape to the natural human inclination to identify holy places, and transformed a domestic space into a temple in which an altar became a place of sacrifice, and Eucharist the sacrificial Mass.

Furthermore, as the basilica took on its medieval form, a colonnaded interior led the eye forward to where God was. Such heavy stress on the horizontal length of the building beckoned the worshiper to take a journey toward a distant goal. This feature, which we might call "pathway," is the distinctive mark of the developed basilica. Medieval Christians did not need theologians to tell them what they could see, that the path was long and could be achieved only by an effort of the will and good works (Norberg-Schulz 1975, chap. 4).

This type of building and its spirituality constitutes the great medieval tradition and comes down to us with many variations, even Puritan-Colonial structures that had little to do with altars, chancels, or other "Roman devices," but substituted an east-wall pulpit instead. And this is the type, reformed and reinforced by the highly influential nineteenth-century Oxford Movement, that inspired the church in Portland and proliferated right through the 1960's, sweeping many denominations and even neo-orthodox theologians like the great Reinhold Niebuhr before it (Bains 2004; Kilde 2002).

The Oxford movement began as an attempt to reform Anglican doctrine in the direction of the ancient tradition but soon grasped the connection between medieval theology and medieval ethos, above all the liturgy and suitable buildings in which to celebrate it. In America the leading architectural exponent was Ralph Adams Cram, a convert from Unitarianism whose credo was a Gothic structure with a long, divided chancel for choir and clergy and an altar at the remote end (Cram 1924). Cram's disciple, F.R. Webber, instructed congregations on how to adapt Gothic architecture to churches of every size and budget (Webber 1937).

A different impulse moved Eastern Orthodox Christians. Drawing on the round buildings used for baptisteries and martyrs' tombs, the East developed the architecturally daring and highly significant structure known as the dome. Constantine himself combined a round building with a basilica in his great monument to the resurrection at Jerusalem, the Church of the Holy Sepulcher. Perhaps because the basilica was so deeply ingrained in Roman society, the greatest early Christian architectural achievement, Holy Wisdom in Constantinople, built by the Emperor Justinian, is still a rectangle, although it mounts to a magnificent dome which appears to float miraculously in mid-air.

The distinctive feature of Eastern Orthodox churches, known ever since for their round domes over rectangular spaces, is what we might call the "umbrella" in contrast to the western "pathway." Whether Orthodox spirituality inspired the dome, or the dome shaped Orthodox spirituality, the two constitute an admirable match. Under its cosmic umbrella the congregation joins with angels and archangels and all the company of heaven to sing the praises of the *Pantocrator*, God made manifest in his Word.

While the classic rectangular shape of the basilica went West, and the dome went East, both retained their fidelity to the basilican family. To extend this generalization even further, while the West always leaned toward works-righteousness along its pathway, a spiritual journey in which God rewards the labors of the penitent pilgrim, the East tended to merge its all-encompassing umbrella with the sacral authority of the realm—what we call, with some exaggeration, "Caesaro-papism."

To return to our observant Martian once more, his field trip to Christian churches would prompt him to summarize the similarities and differences between the two basic church types we have discussed. In the *domus dei*, the temple type, the altar or chancel is "where God is," where pathway is the impulse to action, and where personal devotion responds to awesome mystery. This is Eliade's "sacred space" in Christian architectural form.

White raises three problems with this familiar and beloved building type. It tends to promote the sense that God is utterly remote and transcendent, a God "who dwells somewhere out beyond the east window." It also emphasizes hierarchy by creating unnecessary distinctions between clergy and laity that the liturgy does not require. Finally, its longitudinal pathway toward a distant goal encourages a congregation to become a passive audience that is expected to watch someone else who has been hired to experience God for us (White 2001, 103-104). Its greatest weakness, however, may be its subtle invitation to works inherent in its impulse to spiritual journey.

In the *domus ecclesiae*, the house of God's people, the community gathers around the table, and this gathering is "where God is." It is marked by communion with one another and with God, and by participation in, and celebration of, the Body of Christ in the world. It represents Eliade's "sacred time" since it is essentially domestic, a living-room writ large for a given people with a given tradition at a given moment. Furniture has value only according to its function, including the table needed for the meal and a reading stand for lessons and homily.

This house type was the preference in antiquity, and while few modern churches-in-the-round have proved successful because some in the congregation are always at the minister's back, buildings where people are seated on three sides of pulpit and table have captured the spirit of the type. The weakness of the house church, however, is that it lacks a sense of awe and mystery. One does not feel compelled to fall upon one's knees in prayer, but rather to fall upon one's neighbor in greeting and conversation.

While the twentieth century witnessed some innovative church buildings by great architectural minds such as Frank Lloyd Wright and the Saarinens, Eliel and Eero, we have also endured some interesting shapes—rockets, fish, crowns, and more frequently the ubiquitous A-frames and monumental structures reminiscent of medieval fortresses. These may be fine buildings in themselves, but whatever their style, modern churches may cloud the call to mission until they come to terms with *leiturgia*, what "people do" in worship (White and White 1988), and with the central question in Roger Gobbel's classic essay where he contends that spirituality is not baptism "plus something else." Instead, he concludes, spirituality should ask, who are we and what are we to do this day as baptized Christians in the world? (Gobbel 1980).

But how does all this relate to the bond between space and spirituality? Despite my obvious preferences, this chapter is more than an argument in favor of one form only, the house over the temple. Both types have historical precedent, are rooted in scripture, and reflect perceptions that are precognitive and often unrecognized, so that tampering with either one can create anxiety and a sense of disjuncture (See Rosew 2001).

On the other hand, a comparison between the interiors of Gettysburg Seminary Chapel and St. James Church is illustrative. One is a two-volume structure; the other a three-sided space around the table where no one is far removed from the liturgical action. Yet despite the differences, both demonstrate that by adaptation and creative use of their spaces they can celebrate community and the presence of the incarnate Lord in the midst of his people. Both have struggled to find imaginative ways in which the Word can meet the great and unanswered need of contemporary society for a community that promises wholeness, significant relationships, and ultimate meaning.

We are not dealing simply with bricks and mortar, but with fundamental ways of perceiving God. We are dealing with spaces that form our piety, influence our liturgy, and have an impact on our theology. Church buildings are not neutral. They say something to us as well as about us. They are active spheres in which certain patterns are so profoundly formed that they affect the very way we meet the Lord. Historians have long recognized the truth in the principle, *lex orandi, lex credendi*, spirituality shapes doctrine. Perhaps we should also learn that worship space shapes spirituality.

References
and suggestions for further reading

Giles, Richard Giles. 1999. *Re-pitching the Tent: Re-ordering the Church Building for Worship and Mission*. Norwich: The Canterbury Press.

Gobbel, A. Roger. 1980. "On Constructing Spirituality." *Religious Education* 75:387-473.

Sovik, Edward A. 1973. *Architecture for Worship*. Minneapolis: Augsburg.

White, James F. 2001. "The Seminary Chapel Building as Spiritual Formation." *Theological Education* 38:101-110.

White, James F. and Susan. 1988. *Church Architecture: Building and Renovating for Christian Worship*. Nashville: Abingdon.

Other Works Cited

Bains, David. 2004. "Conduits of Faith: Reinhold Niebuhr's Liturgical Thought." *Church History* 73:168-194.

Banks, Robert. 1980. *Paul's Idea of Community: The Early House Churches in Their Historical Setting.* Grand Rapids: Eerdmans.

Branick, Vincent. 1989. *The House Church in the Writings of Paul.* Wilmington: Glazier.

Christianson, Gerald. 1982. "With Hearts and Hands and Voices." *Lutheran Theological Seminary Bulletin* 62:39-53.

Cram, Ralph Adams. 1914. *Church Building: A Study of the Principles of Architecture in Their Relation to the Church.* Boston: Small, Maynard and Company.

DeSantis, Michael. 2002. *Building from Belief.* Collegeville: Liturgicasl Press.

Eliade, Mircea. 1959. *The Sacred and the Profane: The Nature of Religion.* New York: Harcourt, Brace.

Fenwick, John and Bryan Spinks. 1995. *Worship in Transition: The Liturgical Movement in the Twentieth Century.* New York: Continuum.

Foy, Ray. 1979. "A Study of the Doctrine of the Real Presence and Its Implications for Parish Ministry." Unpublished D.Min. thesis. Lutheran Theological Seminary at Gettysburg.

Grube, Charles. 2004. "Shaping Christian Worship by Shaping Its Spaces." Unpublished S.T.M. thesis. Lutheran Theological Seminary at Gettysburg.

Hammond, Peter. 1960. *Liturgy and Architecture.* London: Barrie and Rokliff.

Hoffman, Bengt. 2003. *Theology of the Heart: The Role of Mysticism in the Theology of Martin* Luther. Edited by Pearl Willemssen Hoffman. Minneapolis: Kirk House.

Kilde, Jeanne. 2002. *When Church Became Theater.* New York: Oxford University Press.

Norberg-Schulz, Christian. 1975. *Meaning in Western Architecture.* New York: Praeger.

Rose, Michael. 2001. Ugly as Sin. Manchester, New Hanmpshire: Sophia Institute Press.

Senn, Frank. 1997. *Christian Liturgy, Evangelical and Catholic.* Minneapolis: Fortress.

Summerson, John. 1970. *Victorian Architecture: Four Studies in Evaluation.* New York: Columbia University Press.

Webber, F.R. 1937. *The Small Church: How to Build and Furnish It: With Some Account of the Improvement of Existing Buildings.* Cleveland: J.H. Jansen.

Past Imperfect:
Spiritual Lessons from Things Left Behind

Maria Erling

The treasures and junk left behind in a family—old photos, books, linens, and tableware—might serve a number of functions in modern homes, some quite different from their original, intended use. A very frayed old rag rug now serves as padding on a bench; the photos from generations long gone mix with snapshots of my children to form a decorating scheme in the kitchen. Hymnals and devotional books in several foreign languages inhabit an old bookcase alongside modern novels. The jumble of old and new on mantles, walls, and tabletops reminds family members and visitors alike that this home re-members the past. The sense of continuity that these items bring to the family lends a sense of stability and permanence in spite of all the job and school transitions, and the actual distance from family members. Hanging on to things in this way makes sense to most people; what is a little harder to appreciate and interpret is the way that these material objects can convey a sense of the past, and how and in what way the items left behind by strangers might give us a window into the world that we all have inherited.

As a historian of the religious life of Americans, I use material objects—devotional books and hymnals, embroidered mottos, old bulletins and Sunday school paraphernalia—as tools to understand the religious and spiritual life of generations long past. It takes considerable imagination and sympathetic effort, however, for students to realize how these inert objects can give them a broader and more sympathetic awareness of the religious and cultural experience of another generation. It is often a family connection to an object that can create a bridge of understanding, but once this link is crafted I find that a much broader world is opened up for the interpreter, and the past becomes much more tangible, focused, and meaningful. I propose that this energy of interpretation, this imaginative involvement with things, is a practice that defines and locates that aspect of the concept of spirituality that involves the sense of connectedness with others, or with meaning, or with the divine. As a Lutheran historian much committed to an incarnational theology, I recognize that a sense of connectedness must be anchored in some way.

Historians approach the past after everything is over. Like gleaners who clean up after a harvest, they sift through the remnants and try to make sense out of things that are no longer in use. As a historian of religious life, and particularly as a committed practitioner myself, I believe there are also important values that can be shared by a careful examination of the religious lives of people. In a day of self congratulatory memoirs, of tell-all media hype, it is more than refreshing to discover the more modest testimony of completed lives and actions, and investigate the results of their pursuits and schemes. The result of such study can temper the overwrought enthusiasm of modern planners who can benefit from the perspective of time.

One cannot master the study of history by memorizing dates, events, and figures, or through analyzing causes and effects. The study of history attempts a broader task: to bring the voices of the past, and things once seen and felt, into a living engagement with the present. To learn to understand the past, and to begin to experience and appreciate the sensibilities people once had to their environment, demands a good deal of imagination and energy. The way that historians learn to observe, understand, and convey the words and feelings of another time involves a deep immersion in the voices and things that reflect the past. This process of getting outside oneself and into a world that is at once strange and familiar demands both discipline in guarding the boundaries of the past, knowing what belongs and what does not, and empathy, an appreciation for the social, physical, and emotional dimensions that people once encountered. These practices define the historical discipline and, I argue, would provide a contribution to the more diffuse and hard to define concept of spirituality.

The energy and work put into learning both to hear and to understand the religious or spiritual dimension in voices from another time and place is yet another dimension to the historian's task, and a richer understanding has emerged, I think, because of some new developments in the field of historical work, involving a kind of modern archeology and investigation of material objects. The kind of historical investigation focusing on the material culture and the way that religious life is lived out and practiced in social contexts expands upon the more linear narrative focus provided by traditional historical accounts of leaders, conflict and institution building. Study of the material and social culture of a time and place tells us that individuals lived in families, enjoyed a social life, and reacted to popular images and entertainments in forming their own religious lives. The objects they used can now be interpreted or read for clues as to the religious and social environment in which subjects lived.

As a scholar of America's religious history, with a particular focus on Scandinavian immigrant communities, I look for ways to learn how immigrant Americans experienced their transition from one homeland to another. To do this I concentrate on evidence in letters or other materials they left behind that can show how they understood and articulated the meaning of their journey to friends and family who stayed behind. Immigrants used letters to describe their strange new surroundings, but since they wrote to people who knew them, they could also use their correspondence to illumine a shared world of meaning now put to the test in a new place. The religious and spiritual dimensions of their remembering become evident in the way that comforts are recalled, and in the way that immigrants put ideas from the homeland to the test. In the churches and congregations they built, immigrants used these memories, ideas, and practices not only as links to their past lives, but also to use in fashioning a new religious and spiritual life in America.

People leave things for me now, things they can no longer read or understand. In church attics and basements, in garages and storerooms of the grandchildren of immigrants are boxes and boxes of books, pamphlets, newspapers, magazines and pictures in a foreign tongue. The boxes contain the left behind debris of a family's foreignness, and in this collection of things lay signs of its involvement in a rich and flourishing ethnic religious culture, now only present as a vague and dim awareness. Learning to read these long dead immigrant languages allows entry into a contained but richly hyphenated Swedish-Danish-Finnish-German-Norwegian-Icelandic-American cultural world. There are stories in these collections, also, that in unintended ways disclose the spiritual life of their people and their times.

The primary schooling of immigrants from Scandinavia into the 1920's included a basic religious education that covered catechetical material, Bible reading, and memorization of several hymn texts. Immigrants who quote hymns, or include pious phrases in their letters don't always quote from the selected verses they had to learn in school; often their choice of sentiment reveals to a modern reader that these travelers were also wandering a bit outside the safe established circles of conventional, or established church devotion. Pious immigrants often had been touched by the revival, and had supplemented their meager religious education with additional reading of devotional material. And they had learned a few new hymns and songs. Gathering dust in attics and mold in basements, these books, hymnals, devotional pamphlets, and picture books, now have migrated into a kind of oblivion since modern American readers cannot read the original language and thus cannot decipher or find any meaning in these worn out books.

In letters where writers quote hymns, express pious hopes in formulaic terms, open and close their letters with wishes for God's mercy and health, you can find the semblance of a shared world view, and reading these letters brings back a time of family adventure and connection. In the tight script and overlapping lines that saved on paper and postage, invented spelling of American words, and the detailed advice to nephews and nieces just setting out for the journey the reader gets a deeper glimpse into the material circumstances in which newly arrived immigrants made their way toward a settled life. In later years immigrant workers sent money home at Christmas and received profuse thanks in return. In many letter collections a pattern emerged of an annual letter from Scandinavian relatives in the fall, arriving in time for the American cousin, son, niece, or daughter to write his or her bountiful Christmas reply.

Letter collections that disclose a pattern of growing separation from home and a contrasting back home dependence upon the successful American who left are rare documentary sources. These letter collections provide only fragmentary evidence about families and the immigration experience, since many letter exchanges abruptly ended when the next migration occurred in the family and members were reconnected in America. Nevertheless, many families were able to maintain such connections and were prudent in saving the evidence. One collection spanned the years of 1887-1953 and several generations. Though these letter collections are not typical of the curatorial practices in most families, modern researchers do have a rich supply of immigrant correspondence to study. Letters and family libraries of books and pamphlets now have migrated to museums and other archival centers and are available to scholars who can compare them and learn much more about the collective immigrant experience.

Hymnals often accompanied immigrants on their journey, and church publishing houses in America made a large proportion of their income by selling them to individuals and congregations. As the immigrant generation passed away and their children began to demand English language resources, immigrant Lutheran denominations began the process of compiling Americanized versions of their hymn and worship traditions. Discarded hymnals are plentiful. They provide a revealing source for investigating the religious lives of these people who negotiated so many transitions. Immigrant letters testify to the way that hymns provided a language to express their religious thoughts and feelings. The world of ideas that hymnals contain and transmit to their users can be interpreted by anyone who devotes some time in concentrated observation. Even hymnals printed in a foreign language can be mined for information. The structure for ordering hymn collections is plain, and the sections containing prayers and service orders can be easily identified. Students can learn how books were used and sense that home devotional use was envisioned by those who produced these volumes.

When a student is aware of the possible use of a hymnal, the actual use of the book lends clues to the spiritual life of the owner. Books that are heavily used have a patina of wear patterns indicating where a hand had rested on the page. A dictionary can assist in providing modest help in identifying the sort of hymn or prayer, e.g., celebration, comfort at the loss of a child, meditation on Christ's passion, and so on, that provided such solace to the individual. Though the interior life of a person is impossible to detect from examining an inert object, the knowledge that a book had been handled often does tell us that a person's religious life did find expression through familiarity with hymns. An Icelandic settler on the North Dakota plains wrote about the way that he was transported through his imagination back to his home congregation in Iceland when on a Sunday morning he was asked to lead a hymn.[24] This leadership post had once before been bequeathed to him when he was a young man just setting out, and the powerful memory of that earlier time, triggered while leading the song of the congregation in North Dakota, brought him to the recognition that such church leadership made him feel each time like a man who was strong and was useful and free. It was the same hymn, and it unlocked his spiritual memory bank. This young man's full maturity was gained in fellowship with other believers who relied on his leadership and shared an Icelander's reverence for the power of poetry and song.

Women came to age, also, in the immigrant church, and one can gain some insight into the aspirations of one young woman who grew to maturity in a Swedish American urban setting by interpreting her hymnal. This item revealed the possibility that religious life could be made fashionable in the city neighborhoods and among the large numbers of young people who frequented the immigrant congregation at the turn of the century. The little velvet-covered *psalmbok* [the Swedish Church hymnal] was given to Ottilia Swenson on Christmas Day, 1892.

The hand-sized hymnal had a metal clasp and metal edges that protected the corners and spine of the little book. It fits easily in the palm of one hand, and in handling it one can sense

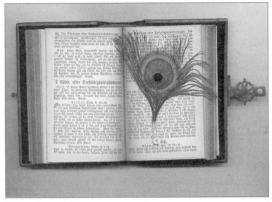

that the owner, Ottilia, carried it with her, hand wrapped around the spine. The velvet is worn very thin along the outside edge of the spine. Similar wear does not seem to have occurred inside the book. It is almost as if Ottilia never opened the hymnal, so fresh are its pages, so limited their wear. There are no soiled edges where finger prints would have inevitably stained them. One cannot, therefore, discover her favorite hymn or prayer by studying how she used several sections of the book. The print in this luxury edition of the hymnal was exceedingly small and only a very sharp-eyed girl could have comfortably read any of the prayers, Sunday lessons, or hymn texts. The Swedish hymnal would have been in regular use at Ottilia's Swedish American congregation in the 1890's. It was not until 1925 that Swedish American Lutherans published as widely used an English hymnal. So the lack of evidence regarding actual use of the interior of the book leaves room for some speculation. Perhaps the lack of finger prints could be explained by the habit of wearing gloves to church, a possibility made more likely by the fact that the book was clearly a deluxe edition of the *psalmbok*. In this case Ottilia may also have opened the book only for hymn singing before closing it again and holding it so that the gilded brass cross would peek out from over her folded hand. The book certainly is an attractive token of fashionable piety. It was not practical or plain enough to be used heavily and did not show signs of heavy domestic use.

Two tokens left behind in random places give additional clues to the nature of Ottilia's relationship with her *psalmbok*. One, a miniature color print of the head of Jesus crowned with thorns, makes a rather stark and dramatic statement. The second item, the top section of a peacock tail feather retains all its glimmering color and the inevitable associations with that bird's vain posturing. These tiny embellishments that showcase a kind of piety reflect in miniature the showy architecture of Lutheran churches built at the turn of the century. Ottilia may not have been a vain woman, but her *psalmbok* communicates the possibility that a pretense of piety may have been a fashionable show during the 1890's.

Ottilia's immigrant church life was not separate from America's popular religious culture; these striving new Americans used their churches both to shape a culture that would preserve their inner world of language and custom, even while they were proud to build impressive structures and show the rest of America how well they could compete. Their sins were not laziness and apathy, but instead sins of ambition and pride, of envy and clannishness. Ottilia's involvement in an immigrant Lutheran congregation did not remove her from America's popular culture.

One can only hazard guesses about the interior life of a person like Ottilia, who was and remains a stranger. Her rather unused *psalmbok* does not give many clues as to her character, anxieties, or hopes. The scattered tokens or bookmarks add more mystery than clarity, and any reconstruction of their meaning can only be partial and is necessarily an effort of the imagination. Fitting these objects into the wider story of immigrant life in congregations, however, gives the historian a firmer grasp on the religious culture they attempt to interpret. Ottilia belonged to a congregation where immigrants met, socialized, worshipped and exchanged gifts. Her religious life occurred in the decorative environment of late 19th century Victorian fashion, and even though she lived in an immigrant community the popular culture of American fashionable piety was very much present also for her. Putting immigrant religious experience in this broader, American popular context also helps modern interpreters to mainstream the immigrant experience rather than to separate it into an enclave of ethnic piety.

Laurel Thatcher Ulrich, in her book *The Age of Homespun*, describes a painted cabinet from a colonial home in New England. She makes the obvious but necessary comment that women's wealth in early American society, unlike men's, had to be portable. Expecting to leave their home and be joined to their husband's family and property, young women who were industrious, and mothers who wanted to pass on their wealth, put their energy and time into making and fashioning things that could accompany a woman throughout her more itinerant life. Thus the weaving, stitching, and embroidering of textiles, and the careful packing and preservation of linen represented transferable wealth—stuff meant to be used as well as handed down to daughters. In immigrant culture in America the portability was relevant to both men and women for it ensured the continuing relevance of religious objects or practices in the new social environment. Buildings and bells could not accompany immigrants, but psalmboks, postils, and pious tracts were packed among the linens in the chests and carried on trains and wagons to new apartments and settlements. Fields and factories were left behind, but traditional foods and festivals, the celebrations that women held in homes, could be maintained. By dint of effort, through imaginative refashioning of American materials, a semblance of home could be recreated in a new place.

One of my grandfathers emigrated with his parents in 1905 when he was still a preschooler. In their collection of photos we have a picture of the young family, still in Denmark, seated in the living room of their apartment. In the photo my great-grandmother is holding a baby while my grandfather is seated on an upholstered sofa. Across the room great-grandfather is playing a reed organ. In the corner of the room is a stuffed owl, the walls are papered with floral patterns, and several house plants and ferns are placed near the windows. The tables are covered with linens and the floors with machine-loomed rugs. The apartment and the activity captured in the photo speak of middle class aspirations, and even a degree of refinement. This is not the home of the poor and landless immigrant that we often imagine when hearing the Emma Lazarus poem: "Send me your tired, your poor, your huddled masses yearning to breathe free. Send these, the tempest tossed to me." This home, by contrast, tells of people who have some means.

What does the room tell of their religious aspirations? Above the window there is a mirror, and it reveals the reflection of an embroidered motto on the opposite wall. In light thread against a black background, portions of a religious motto are legible. Among the possessions distributed among family members from my grandfather's home was a framed hand-stitched motto, in Danish, that had been displayed above the door to his bedroom. It read "Allt af Naade," or, "Everything by Grace," which we all understood meant that all the accumulations of years, the success, the prosperity and happiness of a family, all these things came as a free gift, as grace, and not from work or reward. This motto expressed the belief and at the same time taught my grandfather and his family that the proper response to life's abundance was gratitude, not pride, generosity, not hoarding. "Allt af Naade" was not the same motto that had hung in the Danish living room of his parents. It came from an older parishioner that my grandfather visited when he was her pastor. Stitching religious mottos onto velvet and framing and displaying them was not a unique practice of one family, apparently, but part of a wider cultural practice of decorous pietism. This practice made its way to America and survived several generations. These days I have to translate the motto that hangs above my kitchen doorframe, but I enjoy knowing about the many places it has hung in the past, and the sentiment still teaches me that gratitude is the primary Christian virtue.

In our consumer driven culture that uses things up and watches as traditions go out of style, the useful life of objects is greatly diminished, as is their wealth, gained through labor and honored transfer. "Old fashioned" practices instead become evocative of bygone times and places, gratefully tucked away, along with the painstaking preparations that kept them alive. Modern women and men give no time to making this kind of wealth. Women who worked to make things to pass on may have boasted in their wealth, and needed the tempering spirit of generosity, but ours is a more means-spirited self-involved time of consuming and absorbing things that come unearned to us. We need the witness of these objects to remind us in explicit ways to get beyond ourselves and more involved with a world that needs our work, passion and curiosity, our commitment and not only our consumption.

Posters and advertizing slogans provide that function in our world today, but they tend to lack the generous spirit that adorned pious homes. "Go for it" and "Be all that you can be" announce our culture's obsession with self striving and individual ambition. Religious messages today would not be as popularly appealing, nor would living a religious life be as fashionable as it once was for the Ottilia Swenson's of this world.

The use and reuse of older things, the love of antiques and adventure of finding useful objects in a flea market, all of these practices are not overtly religious, but participate in a kind of spiritual colonizing of the past, an activity that does reflect rather noticeable, if inchoate religious impulses. When my husband and I set up our household, and began to arrange furniture and framed pictures that had been in a grandparent's home, a sense of their presence filled our new place. We imagined their style, and saw in the carpet's wear how grandfather had stood to serve the family meal. The patterns of domestic life were plain to read on these objects—they told of middle class refinement, and betrayed their adoption of a formal and proper manner of life. Our lifestyle has also been affected by the choice to save and use these family things alongside other older finds from antique shops. When I bake and don one of the many aprons from a grandmother's collection, I enter a womanly world not of my making. The presence of these tokens of another time and the sensibilities they convey of another age would be much less forbidding if they were tucked away, unused. The choice to engage them and put them into service, however, connects me and my family with a stream of tradition and practice in a living, active way.

Not all families want to keep such things; they neither read them for the tales they reveal nor use them to create new occasions and memories, but my work as a historian necessarily involves a considerable immersion not only in reading and interpreting, but also feeling the patina of the left behind material world. I contend that it is more than merely an academic interest I hold in these things, but also a practice I keep to weave into my daily life a web of connections that keep alive for me the living work of generations long ago. The home I live in, the floors I sweep, the meals I cook, the books I read, and the papers I write should not be self-contained, or self-directed activities, but are there for the sheltering, nourishing, and enriching of family and friends. The fellowship of Christians extends the table meal of Jesus over and over again to new generations. The impulse to remember and rehearse is not felt as vividly as it can be until real things are taken and touched and seen. Historians who work to imagine the past and to convey a sympathetic understanding are engaged in a kind of practice of spirituality that is incarnational, anchored, connected to real things, and to the world we inhabit.

Pastoral Counseling and Spiritual Direction: Pastoral Theology's Stepchildren?

Norma Schweitzer Wood

In the last several decades those interested in Lutheran theological education have puzzled over whether spiritual direction has a rightful place in the preparation for ministry and what that place might be. Discussions have been fitful as faculties, ecclesial partners and students struggled for a common parlance about the terms spiritual, spirituality, spiritual formation, and spiritual direction. While there has been a growing appreciation for the concept of spiritual formation, both the term and the practice of spiritual direction are still largely held at arm's length out of a lingering suspicion that they might indulge *incurvatus ad se*, a turning in on oneself.

At the same time, the shifting character and viability of pastoral counseling as a congregational ministry have also been under scrutiny. Criticism was rightly lobbed at this discipline whenever it was seen to move in a direction that is too clinically psychological and disengaged from the congregation. Questions arose: Is pastoral counseling a discipline that can and should be taught in a program preparing men and women for parish ministry? Is it too psychological, too much a secular and clinical specialization?

Both pastoral counseling and spiritual direction have their roots in the classic Christian tradition of *Seelsorge* (the care of souls). Pastoral counseling grows out of the healing tradition that speaks of the minister as a "physician of the soul" dispensing medicine for the soul, in relation to the church as a hospital where sinners might go to have sins healed. Spiritual direction is rooted in the metaphor, "counselor of the soul," with its emphasis on matters of discipleship, conscience, self-examination, and confession. And yet the modern flourishing of pastoral counseling and spiritual direction has made them somewhat like stepchildren in the larger family of pastoral care and pastoral theology.

This chapter will rehearse some of this flourishing, identify the distinctive purposes, tasks and skills of each discipline, offer a perspective on their kinship in the family of pastoral care, and affirm their importance to theological education.

Pastoral Counseling

In one sense pastoral counseling stands in an ancient tradition of pastoral care, and in another sense it has not yet achieved maturity. Born within the twentieth century as a new ministry of pastoral care, it was expected to be both scientific and religious. While seeing itself in continuity with traditional pastoral functions of healing, sustaining, guiding and reconciling, this new ministry spent most of the 20th century exploring the terrains of psychiatry, psychology and sociology, hoping to give fresh and relevant pastoral perspective to parishioners' existential concerns—anxiety, guilt, depression, alienation, illness, death, interpersonal conflict, and the like.

By the 1950's pastoral counseling had found a foothold in theological education even while it continued its search for resources from the field of psychotherapy and its rapidly proliferating theories and practices. The range of possibility for pastoral and psychological connections grew during the 1960's and 1970's with an amazing variety: neo-Freudian psychoanalysis, gestalt, self-actualization, self-theory, object relations, family systems, group theory, and cognitive, behavioral, existential, strategic, structural, paradoxical therapies, and still more. Clergy were driven both by fascination with these new therapy possibilities and by a fear that the church would become irrelevant if it did not equip itself to use approaches that promised to address the deep psychological needs of people.

Although these new psychological resources were thought of as servants to ministry, there was still a growing preoccupation with matters psychological. On the one hand, pastoral counseling was emerging as a clinical specialization with more and more start-up centers and private practices that were not related to congregations. Those who wanted to practice as pastoral counselors sought appropriate continuing education, professionalization, the development of licensing procedures, accreditation standards and eligibility for third party insurance coverage. On the other hand, many pastoral theologians were expressing grave concern about what seemed to be an over-psychologizing of pastoral counseling and a consequent loss of Biblical grounding and theological clarity.

Even while these tensions continue to exist, a dominant conversation in the more recent pastoral counseling literature reaffirms and emphasizes its vital connection to pastoral theology, albeit consensus about what that means is yet to be achieved. Today's conversational voices are pluralistic, ecumenical and eclectic in their particular interests and emphases. And, to season things a bit more, pastoral psychotherapy has presented itself as a further specialization of pastoral care.

The pastoral counseling discipline is a stepchild in the family of pastoral theology in the sense that it has some new parents—psychology and professionalization. And as is often the case in blended families, the step-parental roles are still being clarified and defined. Don Browning begins such clarification by setting out two sorts of problems for which people seek pastoral attention:

1) those problems that could be described as psychological blocks and developmental barriers to personal growth. These center on the sorts of intrapersonal conflicts and ambivalence that depress a person's capacity to act freely and assuredly.

2) those that center on values clarification and/or questions of religious commitment. Pastoral care tends to concentrate on values confusion and religious commitment.

Pastoral psychotherapy concentrates on persistent psychological blocks and developmental impediments. Pastoral counseling addresses both sets of problems. All three pastoral approaches utilize religious, ethical and psychological perspectives but differ in their concentrations of effort and in their needs for specialized training (Browning 1993).

Donald Capps differentiates pastoral care and pastoral counseling in their purposeful response to the congregant's story. While all pastoral care involves the telling of stories as people search for meaning and direction in their lives, in pastoral counseling there is a focus on a systematic effort to interpret the stories so that new understandings may occur. In pastoral care the minister responds more in terms of the story's basic factualness; in pastoral counseling, an interpretive approach is expected (Capps 1998).

Christie Neuger lifts up common purposes in pastoral care and counseling: advocacy and empowerment of those who are oppressed and systemically deprived of power (Neuger 1993).

Accordingly, then, pastoral counseling offers care on behalf of the church to those seeking help in resolving conflicts, sorting out value confusions, and addressing issues of freedom and responsibility. Its caring response is shaped as Christian theology is faithfully and judiciously assisted by modern behavioral science resources. More particularly this caring may be directed as guiding, sustaining, healing, or reconciling as it focuses on congregants' self-disclosures of burden and their appeals for relief. The pastoral counseling process offers a "confessional venue" for examining what is painful and oppressive in a congregant's life and, informed by psychosocial resources, interprets that from a faith perspective. A desired outcome of that process is a heightened awareness of the social justice values, in the sense that faith fuels discipleship, and discipleship leads to mission and humanitarian work.

Spiritual Direction

Charles Gerkin sets a context for spiritual direction:

At its best, the theme of spiritual search has expressed the dependence of human life on the mystery of divine grace. Quite apart from the necessity to order human ways of living, all human living is made possible by God's faithful and continuing activity on human behalf. When humans fail, God's forgiveness is mysteriously available. Thus it is by God's grace that human life is empowered, redeemed, renewed and reformed. By God's grace likewise particular gifts of discernment and healing are granted to individuals, graces known as gifts of the Spirit. The Christian community down through the ages has valued and cultivated its spiritual leaders as well as its moral leaders (Gerkin 1997, 86).

Spiritual direction is one response to spiritual searching. It is among the many pastoral forms of guiding believers through the vicissitudes that characterize the Christian life. The Holy Spirit is understood to be the Director, and guidance is mediated by one who listens to another's interior world and guides him or her through prayer, meditation and discernment of God's leading presence in his or her life.

Spiritual direction has historically been associated with the Roman Catholic, Orthodox and Anglican traditions and with priestly formation. Spiritual directors today often lift as models the 3rd century monastic communities and their spiritual fathers and mothers. Troubled Christians went out to the desert *amma* or *abba* to seek healing and a word of counsel from her or him that would address the passions that were getting in the way of loving God and responding to God's will. The main activities for helping were prayer, reading the psalms, with "a word" of guidance or story to address underlying dynamics (Bondi 1986).

Lutheran scholars and believers are in the process today of reclaiming the word "spirituality" in speaking about particular (but not necessarily unique) emphases that are part of the Lutheran tradition's way of nurturing believers into living a life with God. The term "spiritual direction," however, is not as appreciably embraced, perhaps because of its historical associations with personal and inward piety.

Spiritual direction in a sense is concerned with the application of key Christian doctrines to the particular lives of Christians in particular contexts of faith. The focal point of direction is prayer that may be silent or voiced, contemplative or active, expressive or meditative, and is influenced by the language, symbols and perspectives of the tradition of spirituality in which it is situated.

Urban T. Holmes provided a phenomenology and analysis of the rich treasury of Christian prayer tradition that continues to inform the practice of spiritual direction (Holmes 1980). He rooted this analysis in a psychological theory of consciousness and used two intersecting scales: a horizontal scale ranging from emptying prayer (apophatic) to imaginal meditation (kataphatic), and a vertical scale ranging from a speculative aim (illumination of the mind) to an affective one (illumination of the heart). Historical expressions of prayer, then, are viewed through the differentiation of four forms: speculative-kataphatic, affective-kataphatic, affective-apophatic and speculative-apophatic. Holmes believed that in practice these prayer forms should be held in tension with one another to avoid the potential excesses in each when taken in isolation.

The aim of the speculative-kataphatic prayer path is to guide persons in their vocation in the world and is concerned with discernment of God's will, discernment of the spirits, imitation of Jesus, and becoming aware of God's presence and action in the world. It uses expressions of prayer and meditation that engage the imagination, the senses and the intellect to become attentive to God's Spirit working in the lives of directees.

The affective-kataphatic prayer path is part of a sensate, feeling spirituality that aims to achieve holiness of life and is concerned about friendship with Jesus and the outpouring of the Spirit as a sign of God's reign in individual and communal life. It fully engages the emotions and senses both to praise God and to identify with the Way of the Cross.

The affective-apophatic path aims at closeness to God by emptying self of all distractions so as to be fully aware of the Holy Spirit and its activity. Teresa of Avila, John of the Cross, and Thomas Merton are illustrative of this spirituality. Spiritual disciplines may include silence and a space that is not distracted by the senses, or they may use the senses, the icon, music, and incense as windows through which to move beyond senses and connect with the mystery of God.

The speculative-apophatic path is about "doing" spirituality, focusing on obeying God's will, witnessing to God's reign and striving for justice and peace. It is focused on prayer that is active and immediate: How can God's reign come through me now, this day?

Protestantism, with its keynote emphasis on justification, has not been much interested in these spiritual direction resources until recently. Beginning in the mid-1980's a surge of interest in spirituality and a desire for individualized spiritual help manifested itself in our culture. Seekers (not always Christian) perceiving a disconnection between the institutional church and their own lives, were eager to learn about spirituality. Believers, too, began turning to the rich and variegated traditions of spirituality and offered up these resources to those longing for spiritual meaning in their lives. These took forms of retreats, workshops on meditation, contemplative prayer and other spiritual practices. Spiritual direction drew the attention and interest of protestant educators and practitioners during this time.

An ecumenical enterprise was envisioned and carried forward in 1989 at a conference of some 90 spiritual directors at Mercy Center in Burlingame, California. Today it is known as "Spiritual Directors International," with a membership that includes directors from over 50 nations representing multiple social, ethnic and cultural traditions. It is grounded in the Christian faith, and the association serves a growing worldwide network of spiritual directors and the people who train them. Its journal, *Presence: The Journal of Spiritual Direction International* has these aims: "To facilitate professional conversation among spiritual directors and those engaged in the formation of spiritual directors" and "to articulate the essential elements of our practice and training, to encourage accountability, and to develop clear ethical standards" (www.sdiworld.org) As spiritual direction training programs emerged, they too wrestled with issues of identity, accountability and with the relationship of spiritual direction to pastoral counseling.

To my mind, it is not simple happenstance that the surge of interest in spirituality and spiritual direction resurfaced at a time when pastoral counseling was struggling to correct itself from over-psychologization and weakened theological moorings. Moreover, both disciplines have needed to respond to larger post-modern cultural contexts and the tensions around shifting paradigms, hermeneutical methods, multiculturalism, feminism and liberation theologies.

This has been a time when many Protestants, for whom the term "spirituality" was outside their traditional language, began not only plumbing the depths of their own historical practices of piety, but also exploring the resources within the Roman, Orthodox, and Anglican traditions. They turned to the monastic traditions, the medieval mystics, the French Catholic spiritual writers, and the Ignatian tradition of spiritual direction and its spiritual exercise retreats. Spirituality resources for direction also now include a diverse twentieth century reservoir of global and ecumenical writers: liberation voices from Africa, Latin America, Asia, Europe and North America, all pointing to the presence of God in all of life, to reliance on God for power to face life's challenges, and to the importance of discerning how God's Spirit is at work.

Common Parentage

Pastoral counseling and spiritual direction have much in common; after all, the same mother, the Christian tradition, birthed them. However, even with that common parentage, an important distinction can be noted in their beginning "contracts" for work.

While pastoral counseling often begins with a congregant's presenting problem and desire for healing, the congregant may not see how the problem relates to faith or God. In the course of the pastoral counseling process, though, a pastoral aim is to help him or her hear the gospel so to invite such connection to that pain and healing. In spiritual direction the congregant comes with a stated desire to become more aware of God's presence in his or her life and to discern God's gracious purpose. Direction explicitly presupposes that God is present and at work; direction focuses on awareness of God, on recognizing the movements of the Holy Spirit, and helping to make sense of daily struggles in relation to the religious experience of the directee.

The pastoral counselor may embrace these "discipleship" goals, even though they may not be in the mind of the counselee. Instead, some specific problems demand attention. While never forced, during the course of care the pastoral counselor invites the person to explore a religious discernment of that problem. Pastoral counseling has both a healing purpose and a potential for facilitating increased awareness of discipleship. Spiritual direction is focused at the outset on a desire to know

God; in pastoral counseling that purpose may be hidden, implicit and emergent. Still both disciplines assume that all experience can be viewed from a faith perspective. Each uses the Christian tradition in the sifting, sorting and weighing processes that go on as it engages its overall purposes. Each discipline takes seriously the person's emerging life drama in relation to the faith community.

Living in a Blended Family

The term blended family is used to reference the aftermath of remarriage. While it is true that all families change and grow, the blended family expands suddenly and exponentially from one set of parents to include two or even three or four, along with a bevy of step-siblings, grandparents, aunts and uncles. As this expanding network of relationships brings new interests and influences into blended family life, member roles are up for new definition. Everyone adapts to a new context. And role clarity is critical for successful adaptation! It is within this context of expansion and role clarification in the family of pastoral care that pastoral counseling and spiritual direction can be situated.

Those in the pastoral care family share a new epistemological context: post-modern but with emphases that frame life in dynamic and holistic perspectives. Pastoral counseling emphasizes the related self, the self in relationship to familial, socio-political, economic and ecclesial systems. Spiritual direction strives to attend to the web of personal, interpersonal, contextual and global dimensions of life in God.

The new stepparent, psychology, has had a considerable shaping influence, perhaps more so on pastoral counseling than on spiritual direction. Still, the discipline of listening is informed by psychology and is foundational to both disciplines even while it may be focused differently. Both pastoral counselors and spiritual directors must be able to enter into another's world of meaning and experience in order to carry out their disciplines' purposes—healing and discipleship. Psychology has helped both disciplines to learn more about listening to people and to be conversant with their inner landscapes.

Nonetheless, each has also been nurtured in a distinctively flavored family culture: one in a culture of psyche, the other in a culture of spirit. With its emphasis on healing, pastoral counseling has drawn heavily on the parental influences of depth psychology, existential and cognitive-behavioral psychologies as it has tried to "exegete" the human. These psychological and psychotherapeutic perspectives brought language that gives fresh meaning to the anxieties of human finitude, motivation, defense mechanisms and human development. But these psychological perspectives come in non-theological frames and need to be sifted, sorted, and interpreted within a context shaped by Christian hope. With its emphasis on loving God, spiritual direction has drawn on the Christian witness of faith in ways that embrace a broad repertoire in practices of piety and discernment of the Spirit. The well of spirituality is deep; its waters are life-giving, restorative, and offer guidance for those wholeheartedly desiring life in God. But the Biblical witness needs to be heeded: not all spirits are of God. In fact at the heart of spiritual direction is a collaboration to distinguish among the various spirits that seem to beckon in different paths. Some of these spirits masquerade as mental illness, and some mental illness presents itself as of God. It is important for those training in the art of spiritual direction to learn the symptomology of mental disorders, to be alert to the importance of collaboration with appropriately trained pastoral counselors, psychotherapists, and mental health professionals, and to make caring and responsible referrals. Referral is necessary whenever a person evidences a danger to self or others, and where symptoms of psychosis, thought and mood disorders, impaired orientation and the like show themselves. Beyond these necessary referrals, it is advisable to consider referral in the presence of any persistent pattern of maladjustment.

In the course of spiritual direction, the directee may experience blocks or issues that would warrant a responsible referral to a pastoral counselor and/or mental health professional. For example, what might initially appear to be an experience of dryness in prayer life may have connected to it a clinical depression that requires medical intervention. And what presents itself as depression may have dimensions of "a dark night of the soul," a term coined by Teresa of Avila and John of the Cross to describe a stage in the soul's journey during which one may feel utterly cut off from God and a loss of attraction for the usual daily pleasures. Still, solace comes in naming the experience as a waiting period, a time in which God is still at work in one's life despite God's seeming absence.

Spiritual direction and pastoral counseling, then, can be respectful siblings who recognize possibilities for fruitful referral, work in collaboration, and appreciate each other's upbringing.

Alan Jones illuminates the relationship this way:

> Psyche may be said to be the container of spirit in that sound psychological development is the best preparation for spiritual formation. . . . On the other hand there are those who have a rich spiritual life but whose psyche can barely hold life together with any kind of integrity. . . . It is evident that psyche and spirit need each other. In the same way pastoral counseling and spiritual direction are complementary (Jones 1990, 1213).

And so recognition is needed for the mutual and distinctive heritages of these related disciplines. While spiritual direction's primary goal is helping another to discern the presence and leading of God in his or her life, it pays close attention to the social and psychological pressures that shape the interior landscapes of a person's life and to the need for supplemental pastoral counseling work. And while the primary goal of pastoral counseling is to offer a confessional venue in which pains and problems in a congregant's life can be disclosed, made sense of, and faithfully interpreted, it knows that spiritual direction is a rich referral resource for helping congregants in their faith journey and in living out that faith in discipleship.

Both disciplines will benefit from the integrating and guiding eye of a pastoral theology that continues to extend its parental embrace. And theological education will be strengthened as it accords each a valued place in the curricular and para-curricular aspects of the seminary formation of women and men preparing for parish-related ministry.

References

Bondi, Roberta C. 1986. "The Abba and Amma in Early Monasticism: The First Pastoral Counselors?" *The Journal of Pastoral Care* 40/4:311-320.

Browning, Donald S. 1993. "Introduction to Pastoral Counseling." In *Clinical Handbook of Pastoral Counseling*, vol 1. Edited by Robert J Wicks,

Richard D. Parsons and Donald Capps. New York: Paulist Press, 5-13.

Capps, Donald. 1998. *Living Stories: Pastoral Counseling in Congregational Context*. Minneapolis: Fortress Press.

Neuger, Christie Cozad. 1993. "A Feminist Perspective on Pastoral Counseling with Women." Pages 185-207 in *Clinical Handbook of Pastoral Counseling*, vol 2. Edited by Robert J Wicks, Richard D. Parsons and Donald Capps. New York: Paulist Press.

Gerkins, Charles V. 1997. *An Introduction to Pastoral Care*. Nashville: Abingdon Press.

Holmes, Urban T., III. 1980. *A History of Christian Spirituality: An Analytical Introduction*. New York: Seabury Press.

Jones, Alan. 1990. "Spiritual Direction and Pastoral Care." Page 1213 in *Dictionary of Pastoral Care and Counseling*. Edited by Rodney Hunter. Nashville: Abingdon Press.

Field Education:
Rich Soil for Seminarians' Spiritual Formation

William O. Avery

In the Lutheran tradition academic learning and spirituality have always been blessedly intertwined to the mutual enrichment of both. Theological education without spiritual development seems empty, whereas spirituality without the discipline of critical study seems equally empty and unfocused. Lutheranism appears particularly adept at balancing the two. In seminary preparation for ministry, field education is uniquely poised to provide students with opportunities for spiritual development to complement their academic learning. This statement is also the conclusion arising from observations of field education supervisors working with the Lutheran Theological Seminary at Gettysburg.

Surveyed by me through the Gettysburg Seminary's field education office, the supervisors reveal a mosaic of spiritualities both evidenced and encouraged under the rubric of Lutheran theological education. This reveals an enduring strength of Lutheranism: while securely rooted in the liturgical, confessional and scriptural tenets of tradition, field education students, like Lutherans of every age, experience God's grace as the Holy Spirit directing their lives.

One supervisor praised a first-year student for "unparalleled" depth of spirituality that bolstered the supervisor's own experience. The student served in a year in which the pastor saw unexpected congregational conflict and the deaths of two women in their 20's, both of whom were active in the congregation—one from a heroin overdose and the other of a sudden heart attack. "This student prayed for me and laid his hands upon me in our time of prayer in the middle of that difficult time," the supervisor said. "What a witness to Christ's love and the power of the blessing of the Holy Spirit." As this example illustrates, field education provides occasions for deep spiritual sharing among both students and their mentors.

Field education provides a significant proportion of theological education for most students at Gettysburg Seminary, whose main task is to prepare men and women for rostered ministry—as ordained pastors, as associates in ministry or as diaconal ministers. Only those earning a purely academic degree—a very small fraction of Gettysburg's students—are exempt from field education. Candidates for ordination have the most extensive field education: Teaching Parish, seven to ten hours a week, normally during their first academic year; Clinical Pastoral Education, usually full-time for eleven weeks; and twelve months of internship, full-time in a parish. All told, ordination candidates earning the traditional Master of Divinity spend forty percent of their seminary time in field education. Thus, much of spiritual formation occurs there.

To investigate "spirituality in field education," I invited supervisors in teaching parishes, CPE, and internship sites to write two to four pages on "how 'spirituality' is a part of the teaching." I refrained from defining spirituality, but asked them to "describe this concept in whatever way it applies to their ministry situation." Of forty-nine invitations sent out, twenty-six written responses came back, or slightly more than half, which I considered excellent, especially since supervisors had to frame their essay with little direction from me. Essays came from nine teaching parish supervisors, fifteen internship supervisors, and the only two Lutheran CPE supervisors who regularly work with our students. These supervisors play a critical role in the spiritual formation of our students. We consider them to be "adjunct faculty," and they are so listed in our catalog. Moreover, my informal research of several years ago suggests that five years after graduation more students list their internship supervisor than any faculty member as the person who had the most influence on them during their seminary experience. Thus, their input and perceptions are very valuable in assessing how seminary students understand and apply spirituality in their field training and afterwards.

A Lutheran Understanding of Spirituality

1. A non-rooted concept of spirituality makes little sense

None of the supervisors supports a vague notion of spirituality that could be used for both religious and quasi-religious people. One supervisor spoke for many: "*Spirituality* is the 'in' word today in religious circles (and non-religious circles, for that matter), and like most 'in' words, it is used so much and in so many ways as to be almost devoid of meaning." Another pastor said spirituality "has become a loaded term and, as a result, has been diminished as a word of content generally understood and accepted."

A CPE supervisor described how, beginning in the mid-1970's, nurses began to look at the connection between religious beliefs and patient care in hospitals. In the publication of the Nursing Taxonomy in 1982, researchers tried to define spiritual in a functional sense, not as a tool or discipline but as a dynamic principle: "Spirituality is the life principle that pervades a person's entire being—volitional, emotional, moral-ethical, intellectual and physical dimensions—and generates a capacity for transcendent values." Furthermore, "the spiritual dimension of a person integrates and transcends the biological and psychosocial nature" (Kim and Derry, 1982, 332). The supervisor points out problems with this definition: 1) there is still no consensus on what spirituality is; 2) this concept of spirituality is open to misuse by physicians, nurses, and health care administration on the one hand and by pastors and patients on the other; and 3) hospital chaplains are largely kept out of this picture.

The other CPE supervisor wrote that religion needs spirituality or it is a dead and lifeless routine, but the need goes both ways: "Spirituality without a thoughtful theology and sound religious practice has no mooring or roots. Such spirituality seems free-floating. It is not compelling or ultimately concerned. I often observe that it seems to serve a self-centered aggrandizement." An internship supervisor summarized it well, saying the theology of the cross directs spirituality like an engine pulls a train. "How we think of our life affects how we live that life."

A teaching parish supervisor says he hears the phrase "spiritual needs" most frequently, and ministry is about meeting them. "When I was a military chaplain, this was in fact the whole rationale for having chaplains: to meet the spiritual/religious needs of soldiers," he writes. But while there is much talk today of parish ministry meeting spiritual needs, the content of "spiritual needs" is undefined, and therefore this term is not really helpful. In other words, a biblical or confessional spirituality can be far different from the spirituality in American religiosity in general, which, this pastor claims, is often Gnostic in character.[25]

Another pastor observed that many contemporary definitions of spirituality actually distance it from religion. "Too often I have read articles on spirituality that stress that religion is etymologically derived from the Latin *religare*, to bind or to tie. By allegation or implication, religion is subsequently criticized as a form of bondage, an obstacle to freedom. Spirituality, by contrast, is elevated as a positive and superior thing, a form of freedom—though not infrequently a freedom difficult to distinguish from consumerism." This supervisor concluded that to contrast the two concepts in such simple terms diminishes both.

Lutherans, he wrote, understand Christian discipleship as living a paradox: "A Christian is perfectly free lord of all, subject to none [and] a perfectly dutiful servant of all, subject to all" (LW 31:344). Lutherans have "historically had little difficulty with the notion of being 'religious,' i.e. of being 'bound.'" Lutherans also understand that spirituality is itself a word with "an etymological heritage, a notion infused with particularity. Specifically, Christian spirituality is about being rooted in the Spirit." Thus, the pastor defined spirituality as "the way(s) by which we become aware of the Presence of God (or to put a finer point on it, the activity of the Holy Spirit)." Like religion, spirituality has to do with discipline, with practices, with habits. "And like religion, spirituality thus defined has to do with the individual only to the extent that that individual is the member of a larger community, the Body of Christ. Spirituality, whether individual or corporate, has to do with the *pneuma*, the breath of

God, inspiring and enlivening human beings for the purpose of God's presence being made known in the world."

2. Spirituality as God's gift to us

These Lutheran supervisors say emphatically that spirituality is about the Holy Spirit. It is not a quest for God, but God's gift to us. "While much of what passes for religion and spirituality is humanity's attempt to 'find' or 'get' to God or 'aspire' to God-likeness, in the coming of Jesus we have a God who has come to us and is among us and whose presence is there to be discovered and experienced through the gift and power of the Holy Spirit," says one supervisor. He paraphrases Martin Luther to sum up his thought: "Faith is the empty hands by which we receive the gifts of God."

Because spirituality is the gift of the Holy Spirit, many supervisors agree that it begins in baptism. "Spirituality for Lutherans is centered and grounded in grace," reflects one supervisor. "Spirituality is a response to God's mighty deeds in Jesus Christ. Spirituality is therefore centered in Word and Sacrament."

3. Spirituality, grounded in baptism and nourished in worship, has a communal character.

For these supervisors, spirituality's communal and personal elements are both essential. "Spirituality is the living out of the corporate and individual life of the Spirit in the called and gathered community of the baptized," says one Lutheran supervisor.

Again and again these Lutheran mentors ground spirituality in God's gift of the Holy Spirit offered first in baptism and then reinforced in worship, through Word and Sacrament. It is their Lord, not their work—no matter how noble—that justifies, says one supervisor. He continues that it is in worship, the liturgical cycle and the other tasks of parish ministry such as visitation, pastoral care, and administration, that one becomes increasingly aware that "it is not I who lives, but Christ who lives in me."

Or again, "The spirituality of a congregation is most evident through worship. Spirituality runs a connecting continuum between personal and corporate, private and public. Congregations that share a more corporate sense of spirituality are engaged in service with and to the community." Lastly, an internship supervisor claimed that the "communal understanding of the spiritual life is one of the unique experiences available in the parish internship setting."

Spirituality is thus a double movement. In the words of an intern supervisor, "Grounded in God's grace in Christ Jesus and empowered by the gift of the Holy Spirit, Lutheran spirituality is a double movement expressing Christian wholeness: a growth to maturity within; our sanctification in the inner person (mind, body, spirit), and a growth to maturity without; or discipleship and prophetic, or public, witness in the world."

4. Many definitions of spirituality for Lutherans

Given the three points described so far, many definitions of spirituality fit this Lutheran understanding. Or, perhaps better expressed, a Lutheran understanding can lead to broad ranging definitions of Christian spirituality. One pastor said simply, "In the broadest sense of the word, 'spirituality' includes anything having to do with the spirit." Said another: "To me, spirituality is life under God. That is, spirituality includes all aspects of life." While still another warned that we cannot put the concept of spirituality in a box. Spirituality cannot be confined to a certain kind of experience, or one type of discipline, but is God's indwelling in all things—"then we begin to understand the enormity of what God considers spiritual."

I appreciated the pastor who defined spirituality as a dance, with the Holy Spirit leading, and the pastor who described spirituality as "the profound work of God at the center of our lives assisting us in sensing the presence of God throughout creation." He continued, "We are baptized into the death and resurrection of Christ. This we believe. As such it is not we who live, but Christ who now lives in us." Therefore, "all that we do as God's children is under the guidance of God's Spirit." Not surprisingly, one supervisor concludes: "Lutherans have no monopoly upon spirituality and no agreed upon definition of spirituality. What they do have, however, is a shared commitment that faith arises from God as a gift to us."

The Discipline of Spirituality

I am claiming, based on the essays by these Lutheran supervisors, that there is a "Lutheran" way to understand spirituality. That is, spirituality is always understood as God's gift to us of the Holy Spirit not depending on any good work on our part. To be sure, representatives of many other Christian denominations would claim the same. Yet I think that the intensity of the focus on God's grace, as the very heartbeat of Christianity, is particularly strong in the Lutheran communion. This study of Lutheran field educators indicates that supervisors agree on a basic understanding of spirituality in terms of grace. However, there is no unanimity of thinking about the discipline of spirituality which we may have assumed would be the case.

1. Suspicions of specific disciplines

Some supervisors are uncomfortable talking about the word spirituality and reluctant to prescribe disciplines. "I am a bit suspect of our efforts of trying to derive specific mechanisms and techniques for garnering a 'spirituality,'" writes one. Another mentor confesses, "I'm not much of a "spirituality" person. The very term scares the heck out of me!" Later he admits that he personally is not given to spiritual retreat or to times of silence. "I am much more of a Brother Lawrence[26] kind of person who sees the Spirit at work in activity and movement." This pastor continues, "But I do understand the need for any congregation to live with a sense of God's presence, and we do cultivate that spirit through worship, sense of community, word and sacrament, adult learning experiences, daily devotions, money for people who want to go on retreats." For this pastor, the main thrust of spirituality in the congregation is through the regular celebration of the Eucharist.

Another pastor offers, "I think we can hold up the idea of a liturgical spirituality, a personal mode of apprehending the gospel and its effects in which the Church's public celebration of Word and Sacrament is central." This pastor sees the discipline of Morning and Evening prayer "as the simplest and most direct way of structuring prayer and spirituality. This would contrast very starkly on the one hand with a pietistic emphasis on personal and improvised prayer (though it is surely not in stark conflict with it) and on the other hand with the amorphous sentimentality that is widely confused with spirituality."

2. Spiritual formation

Several pastors framed spirituality in the context of "formation." For one pastor who spoke extensively on this point, formation is "the overriding principle that governs the whole of our life long process as Christians, to form and mold us into the image of Christ Himself." He believes that this concept "is not easy but rather is demanding and time consuming and requires of us everything that we have to give." It has fallen into general disregard within the Church, "as we have looked for easier ways to entice membership in our congregations and to make fewer demands on our members when they are there." In contrast, this pastor looks to the sense of community in Acts 2, where "in the breaking of bread, fellowship, prayer and worship they were formed into the likeness of the Body of Christ itself."

Formation, therefore, should be an integral part of the learning process that students enter when they come to seminary. This pastor examines the implications: "All large institutions have a process of formation, whether it be military, church, prison, etc., in which the person is broken down, in which they lose their own identity to a greater or lesser degree and in which they are then built up into a new identity which conforms to the objectives of that institution." This formation requires "a whole new world view. It requires that we bend our wills to the will of God, something that we, in our sinfulness continue to oppose, thereby falling into the age-old rebellion of idolatry."

Formation, he continues, requires rigorous training of self in the spiritual disciplines—for example, a strong prayer life as well as learning mechanisms, such as meditation, that support prayer life. It calls for study of those who have, through the centuries, written about the pastoral office and what that means today. This pastor insists students pay careful attention to their spiritual life so that when they get into difficulties in the parish, they will be less inclined to rely solely on their academic learning. "Rather, it is only an understanding of their own relationship to Jesus Christ that is going to help them, and it is only a reliance on His Spirit which is going to give them the strength to see them through the difficulties." While Christianity is indeed relational—beginning with God's relationship to us, I see spirituality as including the integration of theological, academic, intentional learning and practices into a whole. Most Lutherans would not, for example, set spiritual formation over against academic learning.

3. Modeling spiritual disciplines

Except for spirituality grounded in baptism and centered in Word and Sacrament ministry and prayer, none of the pastors claimed that their students must undertake specific mechanisms to enhance spirituality. "There is a wide and rich diversity of spiritual disciplines and practices which have been and continue to be utilized within the Lutheran faith," says one pastor. "Such openness is a direct result of the fact that Lutheran spirituality is not dependent on a particular piety or devotion, but rather on its emphasis on the grace that flows from the death and resurrection of Jesus Christ. To strive for or insist on particular devotional methods or techniques in a manner that suggests they are the correct way or approach runs the serious risk of impeding or replacing the purity of the Gospel."

But the supervisors agreed that spirituality requires discipline. One mentor likened it to studying music seriously. "In my teaching, preaching, and caring ministry, the rote discipline needed for success in music has given way to hard work, dutiful diligence and faithful prayer," she writes. "In these actions I await, look for, and expect the Holy Spirit to enter in, to lead, to intervene, to chasten, and to enrich my life and my ministry." Note how this transfers to her work as supervisor: "Students are invited to pay attention to where the Spirit is working in our relationship as student and mentor, in our congregation, and in our surrounding community."

While a few supervisors were afraid of the word spirituality, several claim Lutherans do not take spirituality as seriously as we could. One noted that few spirituality books are authored by Lutherans: "Are we Lutherans concentrating too much on head versus heart?" Another supervisor acknowledged that "spirituality" is new to many Lutherans, but "piety" is not: "There is a similar meaning of these words in that both are concerned with how faith is lived out in the world, and how faith is shaped by the Church." The use of "piety" rather than "spirituality" would possibly help some Lutherans engage this subject. In my opinion, though, piety has a somewhat loaded connotation today among Lutherans, where it is often understood to mean a focus on personal religious experience and devotional practices.

While some supervisors were leery of prescribing spiritual disciplines, many spoke easily about their own practices. One pastor said that prayer as a response to the grace-filled Word of God was the key to his sense of Lutheran spirituality. But prayer itself, he said, arrives as a response to the promises we receive and discern through reflective study of Scripture and through the life we share as the priesthood of all believers. "Therefore a biblical literacy must go hand-in-hand with any discipline dealing with spirituality," he said. This supervisor sees his role as providing one model of spirituality among many that the seminarian will experience.

One supervisor explained how field education helped her intertwine academic learning and spirituality. According to the mentor, spirituality begins with questions dealing with the depths of the soul. She asks these questions, "What is God doing in my life? Who is God calling me to be? Where do I notice God's presence in my congregation? What is God stirring up? How might I be getting in the way of what God is doing? What do I hear God saying in the assigned scripture? To me? To the congregation? How is God calling me to risk? To watch and listen? To respond in love?" These questions are related to the more academic, official questions of the teaching parish conversations: "What is my understanding of call? What is the role of the pastor/AIM/deaconate? What are the characteristics and history of the teaching parish congregation? What is my leadership style?"

The pastor described her own wrestling: "When I was a seminarian, I could never answer the more objective questions, unless I was also dealing with the more personal questions that begged me to notice the connection between myself and God, the 'spirituality" questions." She sees spirituality deeply interwoven in the teaching parish experience of students. "I invite our soul's journey to be a part of our academic process together."

These convictions inform her interactions as supervisor. "I meet with the student regularly, in a quiet setting. We usually begin with a time of silence, a prayer for openness, and then we read to each other a passage of scripture, often twice. We then reflect and discuss what we hear God's word saying to us." Later they address the weekly assigned topic. "Nevertheless, these more academic questions and discussions still seem to be grounded in our beginning promise: listening to what God is doing and saying." Second, in meeting with students the pastor is open and honest about her own journey with God, including her own struggles. "If I portray myself as the 'expert' and the 'experienced pastor,' then I deny the students the opportunity to see how I must trust God's leading on a daily basis." Third, she listens to what God is doing in the life of each student knowing that "God is stirring up different challenges for each." She concludes: "The spirituality within teaching parish is very simple, yet very demanding."

Another internship supervisor defined spirituality as "the process of attending to God's presence in life and integrating faith with the business of living." For him, this happens in the pulpit. "Preaching functions as spiritual formation as the pastor is given the responsibility regularly to reflect on the biblical text and how it relates not only to his or her personal life, but also to the corporate life of the congregation." Preaching happens in the dissonance at the intersection between the world as imagined in the text—permeated by the presence of God—and the day-to-day life of parish ministry in which we wonder if and where God is working.

Referring to Walter Brueggemann's writing, this supervisor observes that preaching is no longer a matter of offering theological absolutes. "It is testimony to what God has done in our lives as Christians, what God has done in the life of the congregation, and confession as we recognize that our lives are not all that God intended. It is not a lecture about the text, it is not scholarly reasoning, nor is it, strictly speaking, an argument. It is personal witness to the God who has changed the life of the one preaching and will, in the event of hearing, also change the listener" (See Brueggemann 2000, 49-55). Preaching is a powerful act of treason against the dominant culture to remember that God has freed slaves, sided with the marginalized, healed the sick and raised the dead.

As a subversive enterprise, preaching cannot interpret a text as an object of study where the pastor is safe. "Preaching, as an act of spiritual discipline, puts the preacher and the community squarely in the text, in the world where God acts to change." Preaching is a return to a form of prophecy, because "the preacher will need to have the audacity to speak for God instead of about God." Concludes this pastor, "Much of my work with interns has been to ask them to reflect on how their life and biblical text intersect and to make that a part of their preaching ministry. I have found preaching to be a public spirituality that serves the community, rather than a personal spirituality that serves the self. It is a spirituality of vulnerability and risk as we dare to imagine what God is up to and share it with the worshipping community."

Another supervisor conceives of spirituality from a mind-body-spirit perspective. She observes that Lutherans are very good at the intellectual aspect of faith, coming to know Christ through head knowledge. Knowledge is important. But dealing with spirituality is equally important. In teaching, an intern learns to impart not only content but a spiritual framework for that content. Teaching then becomes a part of spirituality because it connects with God and helps others connect with God in a practical way.

This supervisor also wants interns "to be aware of their bodies spiritually" by taking weekly time away from the office and phone, exercising regularly, eating properly. She learned that how one's spirit is best nurtured varies from intern to intern. "I model some of the ways God feeds my spirit: lighting a candle as the symbol of Christ's presence while I work in the office, listening to meditative music at the office, journaling, and making time to sit in the sun or in a nature setting and just 'be.'" Finally, she notes that her interns' and her own spirits have been fed by the regular practice of "praying through the church membership rolls." The interns mailed letters to three households per week, letting them know when they would be praying for them and seeking any specific prayer requests. "Not all respond, but those who do invite us into their lives and see us as God's representative for them."

Reflecting on spirituality, one supervisor considers what Albert Schweitzer wrote in *Memories of Childhood and Youth*: "Hence I always think that we all live, spiritually, by what others have given us in the significant hours of our life" (Schweitzer 1931, 67). On the one hand, this suggests to the supervisor that "we are the beneficiaries of a vast collection of sacred teachings and faith practices." On the other hand, in the parish internship experience, the intern must engage "not only the active faith stories of the present, but also the rich heritage of the past. The intern is truly the beneficiary of all kinds of blessings and gifts from these saints of old, whom she or he has never met, and will never meet. Having the opportunity to engage these faith stories, share in their wisdom, and experience the joy and hope inherent in them, is an invaluable resource of strength for the intern." Also, in the parish the intern is exposed to how "ordinary saints" have lived out their faith and used the disciplines and practices of faith. "Part of this . . . is also the need to identify and come to grips with the secular religiosity, which often is intertwined with the more orthodox aspects of a believer's faith life." The supervisor, this pastor continued, is the resource person "for assisting the intern in his or her interpretation and understanding of this mixture of both orthodox spiritual practices and public square spirituality."

Finally, one supervisor reflected on how she hoped that internship would deepen a student's spiritual formation in the following ways. The intern would:

- Practice the art of paying attention
- Develop a daily/weekly/yearly rhythm of prayer and study, community and solitude
- Cultivate a discipline of daily personal prayer (whether the liturgical prayer offices, lectio divina, intercessory prayer, contemplative centering prayer, etc.)
- Learn how to worship even while leading worship
- Establish priorities and focus on what is truly needful
- Be ever more richly nourished by the means of grace
- Refine appropriate and wholesome boundaries
- Keep learning how to live with finitude and disappointment, loss and failure
- Grow deep roots that will withstand the dry times
- Keep learning how to trust more in God and less in oneself
- Become more open to the surprises of the Spirit
- Cultivate the wariness of serpents and the innocence of doves
- Maintain a robust sense of humor and a robust sense of awe

To encourage these, the supervisor makes a point to discuss prayer and spiritual life with her students. "We talk about our experience with devotional reading, communal and private prayer, spiritual direction and retreats. We talk about ways we find spiritual nurture and balance, even in the midst of hectic schedules and endless 'to-do' lists. We talk about our experiences of preaching and worship leadership, of pastoral visits and meetings, of teaching confirmation and adult Bible studies," she writes. "We might talk about biblical interpretation or systems theory, about sacramental theology or about various difficult social issues." In so doing, the supervisor and intern reflect on how they experience grace and renewal, and a sense of the holy.

Conclusion

Field education supervisors contribute a significant portion to students' spiritual formation during their time in seminary. These supervisors see the relationship itself as a place of spiritual development for both interns and supervisors. "Intern and supervisor in a relationship of trust and mutual growth are steeped in a rich and rewarding spiritual endeavor," said one, adding, "While together they do many 'spiritual things'—pray, teach, read and study scripture, preach. At a much deeper level the relationship itself is a place of spiritual development for each." While the spiritual disciplines vary considerably, supervisors understand their responsibility to act as coach or mid-wife, creating conditions where the student can explore ways of being open to the Spirit. Unlike the general population who may hold vague notions of spirituality, these supervisors see spirituality as having a specific content that they view through their own lens but based in core Lutheran theology. That is, spirituality is God's gift to us grounded in baptism and enriched by worship and prayer. While there is a very personal side to spirituality, it is grounded in a communal experience and results in a public outcome—building up of the communities of the church and world. Finally, the Lutheran tradition has always intertwined spirituality and learning in a mutually giving way so that both are enhanced.

References

Brueggemann, Walter. 2000. *Deep Memory, Exuberant Hope: Contested Truth in a Post-Christian World.* Edited by Patrick D. Miller. Minneapolis: Fortress Press.

Kim, Mi Ja and Derry Ann Moritz, eds. 1982. ASpiritual Diagnosis Taxonomy." Pages 332-335 in *Classification of Nursing Diagnosis: Proceedings of the Third and Fourth National Conferences.* New York: McGraw Hill.

Luther, Martin. 1520. "The Freedom of a Christian." Pages 333-377 in *Luther's Works*, vol 31. Edited by Harold J. Grimm. Philadelphia: Fortress Press, 1957.

Schweitzer, Albert. 1931. *Memories of Childhood and Youth.* Translated by C.T. Campion. New York: MacMillan Co.

Spirituality, Religious Education, and the Religious Educator

Nelson T. Strobert

The Context

At the time of this writing, there are wide-ranging discussions on television talk-shows, cautioning words from the pulpit, and invigorating exchanges among youth and adult discussion groups in congregations over the release of another Hollywood version of the passion and death of Jesus. These discussions and debates have taken place not only within the United States but also in similar formats abroad. Enthusiastic supporters, movie critics, and skeptics alike have been surprised by the large audiences that have come to see the movie which has broken attendance and revenue records. In addition to church groups buying blocks of tickets, there are large numbers of adolescents and young adults who flocked to the movie screens. Many of these young people would not be seen on an average Sunday morning in an average Christian congregation's worship.

There are a couple of things that can be said about this phenomenon. First, the general public is interested in religion and religious topics in the media. Second, people young and old continue to search for and are interested in the spiritual or theological issues which challenge them in daily living within their homes or workplaces.

We know that one of the top-rated television shows which recently completed its run dealt with angels or messengers from God interacting with humans in the day to day trials of living. A new television series deals with God appearing in different human forms, using a human to interact with the world. In addition to television and the cinema, one can go into any bookstore, in a mall or independent distributor, and find a section on spirituality. Over the years the numbers of bookshelves with this topic have expanded. All of this is to say that "spirituality" is in the news, expanding every day, and attracting people who are active in congregations as well as those who are seeking from outside church circles. With the openness and popularity of these spiritual issues, one must ask several questions: What is spirituality? How do we define the term? How does it develop across the life-span? This essay attempts to address these questions on spirituality by summarizing selected literature and thinkers on spirituality, examining developmental issues, and suggesting possible strategies for lifelong spiritual development in religious or Christian education for the religious educator.

Defining the Term

What is spirituality? To begin addressing this question I recently entered "definitions of spirituality" into an internet search engine. The return from the search gave 451,000 responses or sites. This initial result certainly concurs with Iris Cully who stated that "[s]pirituality may be described but not readily defined, for the boundaries are broad" (Cully 1984, 198). A review of selected literature might help us to get a narrower grasp of the issue.

Thomas Groome in "The Spirituality of the Religious Educator" gives a holistic description of spirituality when he writes: "Spirituality is our conscious attending to God's loving initiative and presence in our lives, and to the movement of God's Spirit that moves our spirit to commit ourselves to wholeness for ourselves and for all human kind by living in right relationship with God, ourselves and others, in every dimension and activity of our lives" (Groome 1988, 10). John Westerhoff in *Spiritual Life* describes spirituality for teaching and preaching as "ordinary, everyday life lived in an ever-deepening and loving relationship to God and therefore to one's true or healthy self, all people, and the whole of creation" (Westerhoff 1994, 1). Marc Lienhard sees a two-fold dimension of spirituality comprising personal piety and at the same time connected with the sacred texts and liturgical life of the community: "We understand by spirituality, at the same time personal piety, as walking by faith, and the texts and the rites, which in the worshipping community or in individual prayer, nurish and direct spirituality" (Lienhard 1997, 1; translation mine)

Scholars utilizing a multicultural perspective have also contributed to defining spirituality. Peter Paris in *The Spirituality of African Peoples* describes spirituality as an integrating factor in the life of religious people. He states, "[t]he 'spirituality' of a people refers to the animating and integrative power that constitutes the principal frame of meaning for individual and collective experiences. Metaphorically, the spirituality of a people is synonymous with the soul of a people: the integrating center of their power and meaning" (Paris 1995, 22). This integrative power is expressed as well by Jonathan Jackson when he writes:

A life story that centers on Christian spirituality is communal. This communal dimension is sorely needed in the present busy, individualistic, competitive society in which we live, where families cease to eat together, neighbors don't know one another, and the struggle for economic sufficiency and gain prevails. We need desperately to recognize and affirm the interconnectedness of our families and communities, local and global and to recognize the necessity of our reaching out toward one another (Jackson 2002, 162)..

Leon McKenzie in forming a developmental approach to spirituality sees it in the framework of a creature focused on ultimate concern:

Spirituality . . . refers to nothing less than a theory of human existence, a theory founded on the dynamics of ultimate concern, a theory that functions as a ground for a particular mode of being-in-the-world. The two principal elements of this description—the notions of theory and ultimate concern—require elaboration.

Spirituality refers to a particular mode of being-in-the-world, a definite way of living. This mode of being-in-the-world is an instantiation of a spiritual vision that is mediated by language descriptive of that vision. A person's spiritual vision, in turn, is shaped to a large extent by the individual's unique perspective and by the values the person brings to the perspective. . . .As a basic minimum, spirituality implies ultimate concern (McKenzie 1985, 49).

From these selected descriptions it can be seen that when one describes the term spirituality, one is engaged in a reflective, integrative, communal as well as personal process. Spirituality utilizes and incorporates the sacred textbooks of the church (the Bible and ancillary resources from the Christian tradition). Furthermore, spirituality is part of an ever deepening relationship with God. These elements seem to indicate that spirituality is more than, and not limited to, an interior or inner experience. It is operational or carried out by the individual in the midst of his or her relationship to the community of believers who continually reflects on his or her relationship with God.

The present writer has been strongly influenced by the critical appraisal of A. Roger Gobbel in an essay entitled "On Constructing Spirituality" (1980) For Gobbel, the term spirituality "is so ambiguous, lacking in clarity and precision and pointing to nothing, that it confuses and confounds while assuming to give clear direction and guidance." He further states that when the term is used by many individuals it is "frequently described as if it were some dimension to be added to the Christian life or 'some thing' to give completion to Christian life." Spirituality as an "added dimension" is something that Gobbel finds annoying, for it denies the centrality of baptism and "it offers the beginning point for the development of a scale to judge the quality or worth of individual Christian life (Gobbel 1980, 411). Gobbel's assessment of the term is also supported in the work of Leon McKenzie who, writing five years later, exclaimed that the term as it has been used by many religious educators can be summed up as superficial thinking, narcissistic pursuit of perfection, self-absorption, and skills or techniques for spiritual improvement (McKenzie 1985, 45).

Gobbel proposes a three-fold definition of spirituality. Christian spirituality is "life lived under and interpreted by the Christian Gospel." This definition emerges from on-going reflection and response to the question, "What does it mean for me this day to be a Christian, to be a baptized person?" The third part is the question asked by the individual in relationship to the community of believers, "What is it to be Christian together in community and in the world?" (Gobbel 1980, 412-413). These are lifelong questions and assume that the human creature is a thinking creature.

Gobbel's definition is a constructivist viewpoint, that is, it is primarily focused on the cognitive development of individuals and how they make sense or meaning for their lives. That is to say that the individual has to make sense out of the data that is presented to or surrounds him/her. Lest one assume that this is really an individualistic manner of living, Gobbel is quick to say that the individual is not self-centered and doing his or her own thing but receiving data from outside of him or herself and interacting with it. If this is the case, then spirituality is not a static position but a dynamic enterprise of the Christian life. Moreover, this also indicates that there is no one way of being involved with or living the spiritual life, for it is going to change as one makes sense out of the continuing data or information, events, and experiences of life (Gobbel 1980, 414). This perspective develops from the work of Jean Piaget, the Swiss developmentalist (see Sigel and Cocking 1977).

In support of the work of constructivists like Gobbel there has emerged a growing body of literature on brain research through work in neuroscience (Jensen 1990; Larsen, 2000). The work of Barbara Bruce in *Our Spiritual Brain* (2002) has been popular with religious educators and practitioners. Recognizing the interdisciplinary nature of brain research, she hones in on what the brain does best, that is, learning. After brief descriptions of the metaphors used to describe the manner in which the brain functions, such as a wax tablet on which impressions are made, a muscle which must be exercised, the factory model, etc., she then turns to develop her own operating model which she calls "information processing." This model incorporates three steps:

◆ Stimulated by what one sees, hears, smells, touches (sensory memory)

◆ The stimulus gets sorted (working memory)

◆ And stored for retrieving (long-term memory) which leads to understanding.

Bruce states that the brain decides what is important to retain and to discard by two factors: does it get the attention of the learner, and is the learner emotionally attached to it. The brain is designed to respond to the stimuli that have emotional connections. From this she says that it is important for the religious educator to be aware of these factors in order to do critical teaching. That is to say, students are responding to what is going on in their lives and will respond to the lesson as they perceive it relating to their lives. Those involved in religious education can assist students in their lives within the Christian community and outside in the general community by providing an environment that presents and challenges the students' brains. Religious education teachers have the ability to help students travel their journey in faith and make life-changing decisions by preparing an environment that is filled with quality and quantity of theological concepts (Bruce 2002, 43; 44).

Can this spiritual journey happen in the lives of the students within the Christian community across the lifespan? Let us examine what might be done educationally to promote and foster a developmental perspective to spirituality through the Christian lifespan.

Young Children

For children from the age of two through five years who are in the pre-operational stage of cognitive development, we can provide a place or environment of safe space and love. They can come to see and experience the church where there is a sense of belonging and where they hear stories about God's love for them in words that are understandable. Visual aids are used to stimulate their thinking about God and God's love and care for them. Children are also excited and find enjoyment in participating in the faith community's celebrations such as Christmas and Easter programs and events. They are learning and experiencing their life within the Christian community. Children at this age level concentrate on time in the present (See Cully 1984, 127; Sigel and Cocking 1977, 59; de Bary 2003, 34-35).

Lower Elementary School Children

In the early years of schooling children are in the concrete operational level of cognitive development where they are developing logical reasoning skills. For their spiritual development teachers need to make intentional associations of the stories in the Bible to the everyday experiences of these young people. They are interested in knowing who they are and to whom they belong in the community of faith. The stories need to be reinforced from a variety of ways, and teachers should give children time to reflect on what they have done and what they have heard. They are also dealing with issues of right and wrong actions, of what is fair and what is unfair (See Cully 1984, 129; Bruce 2002, 45; Sigel and Cocking 1977, 65).

Older Children

At this stage of development, older children are beginning to question the stories and statements that they have heard and consumed over the past years. They may not accept the explanations given to them. They are also interested and watchful of those who are involved in the teaching ministry who model what is being taught to them (See Cully 1984, 130; Bruce 2002, 45; de Bary 2003, 35). This is an important factor in recruiting for teachers for this age group.

Transescents (Younger Adolescents) and Adolescents

From the almost stable years of childhood comes the storm and stress of the transescent (younger adolescents) and adolescent years. This age group is able to do hypothetical and abstract thinking. These young people are going through rapid physical, emotional and intellectual development. While they are able to retain a greater amount of information within their memory banks, they are still developing. These young people can be encouraged and supported in doing service projects. The projects might assist them to reflect on the global nature of God's action in the world. At the same time these young people are separating themselves from their families as they come to claim their own identity. While they seek individual freedom, it is important for them to recognize that they are interdependent persons. In terms of their cognitive development they are at the beginning of the formal operational stage (See Bruce 2002, 46; Cully 1984, 132; Sigel and Cocking 1977, 88).

Adulthood

Development does not stop at the end of adolescence. As the person moves through childhood, transescence, and adolescence, growth continues into the young, middle and older adult years. Part of that growth is spiritual. With the increased number of years, adulthood indicates the differentiation of experiences. Adults are more complex human beings. The spiritual growth in the young adult years may include associations and involvement with religious communities that are different from one's involvement in the earlier periods of life. The middle years of adulthood can bring on the realities of living. Life with or without children, married or unmarried, the care and death of parents, these stand out as some of the critical and often shared experiences of this segment of adulthood. There is a clearer understanding of the suffering of Israel and the agony of our Lord Jesus Christ. This is not a period of warm fuzzies but realistic engagement with the ebb and flow of life (See Cully 1984, 135; de Bary 2003, 39).

The older adult is looking to another phase, the end of their life stories. The years remaining are fewer than the years that have passed. Spirituality at this point in the life-span is reflecting on one's relationship with God that has been nourished through the past years. Their hope is in the promise of God for their lives. They are able to help themselves and others in their individual and corporate remembering (See Cully 1984, 135; de Bary 2003, 40; Johnson and Strobert 1997, 68).

Spirituality and the Religious Educator

Having examined the definition of spirituality in selected literature and considered the variety of spiritual issues through the life-span, what do these elements leave for the religious educator? What is the responsibility of the religious educator, the Sunday School teacher, and the catechist? In the view of this writer, to be the religious educator is to assist the learner in on-going theological reflection. This means that they are steeped in the Word of God. The religious educator attends to the Word of God, interprets the Word of God, and responds to the Word of God (McKenzie 1985, 56). All three components of responsibility correspond to Gobbel's definition and questions for the baptized person in general. For the Christian that means being steeped in the textbook of the church, being readily open to prayer, and worship. In all three this means being involved in the interpretive task. More specifically, the interpretative task and reflection on the work takes place in the various aspects of the religious educator's life. McKenzie includes the following areas of responsibility for the religious educator: Content Specialist, Curriculum Developer, Administrator, and Counselor (McKenzie 1985).

Within the Lutheran tradition, one of the ancillary texts for the education of the people has been Luther's *Small Catechism*. With the clear call for on-going reflection I use the catechism as one way of demonstrating the on-going reflection of the Christian. It is not enough just to memorize the words; one needs to reflect on them. In the required religious education classes for pastoral, associates in ministry, and diaconal candidates the sessions always begin with a few minutes of reflection by utilizing the *Small Catechism*. Hearing the words of Luther, reflecting and responding to the question, "What does this mean [as a baptized person of God]?" assists students in reinforcing as well as interpreting for themselves God's promise of eternal life. Sometimes the responses to the reading and reflection are elaborate, sometimes less so. But although we do not complete the whole book students begin to see demonstrated Luther's words from the preface to the *Large Catechism*, "I must still read and study the Catechism daily, yet I cannot master it as I wish, but must remain a child and pupil of the Catechism—and I do it gladly" (Luther 1529, 380). This is the key to catechetical instruction in particular and religious education in general—ongoing study and reflection on the Word.

Luther goes on to say:

> Therefore, I beg these lazy-bellies and presumptuous saints, for God's sake, to get it into their heads that they are not really and truly such learned and great doctors as they think. I implore them not to imagine that they have learned these parts of the Catechism perfectly, or at least sufficiently, even though they think they know them ever so well. Even if their knowledge of Catechism were perfect (though that is impossible in this life), yet it is highly profitable and fruitful daily to read it and make

it the subject of meditation and conversation. In such reading, conversation, and meditation the Holy Spirit is present and bestows ever new and greater light and fervor, so that day by day we relish and appreciate the Catechism more greatly (Luther 1529, 381).

The power of the catechism was brought home to me when I was a vicar in St. Croix, U.S. Virgin Islands. My supervisor would visit an older adult who was terminally ill. She was not always coherent or verbal. When she did speak, from her lips were the words of Luther's *Small Catechism*, learned many decades before but still near to her cognitively and affectively. Though she had learned the words as part of her confirmation process, the words were such that they were still able to nourish her even in old age. I am also reminded of my paternal grandmother who at 96 years of age continues to finish her day by reading and meditating on Luther's *Small Catechism* as part of her daily devotions. Such reflecting, reading, and meditating suggest that Christian spirituality is a dynamic process.

Conclusion

In a recent conversation with Roger Gobbel, I asked him if his thoughts on the subject of spirituality had changed. "No, I have not changed my mind on the matters in that article. I think that I have fleshed out some things a bit more." He went on to say: "Conversations with each other in community, challenges of each other asking what this day might call us to be and do, worship, liturgy, preaching, etc., are parts of that conversation. Here is the role of adult education." Finally, Gobbel asserted what he had stated 24 years ago: "A Christian's spirituality is the process of living out our baptism."

The religious educator can make no better contribution to the spiritual life of the baptized than to assist people throughout the lifespan to reflect on the graciousness of God who comes in baptism and the rest of our lives. That has been my hope as an educator in the church. For all those involved in educational ministry, pastors, Associates in Ministry, Diaconal Ministers, Sunday school teachers, catechists, this perspective on spirituality might well assist us as we embark on these beginning years of the twenty-first century.

References

Bruce, Barbara. 2002. *The Spiritual Brain*. Nashville: Abingdon Press.

Cully, Iris V. 1984. *Education for Spiritual Growth*. San Francisco: Harper and Row.

De Bary, Edward O. 2003. *Theological Reflection*. Collegeville: Liturgical Press.

Gobbel, A. Roger Gobbel. 1980. "On Constructing Spirituality." *Religious Education* 75:409-421.

Groome, Thomas. 1988. "The Spirituality of the Religious Educator." *Religious Education* 83:9-20.

Jackson, Jonathan. 2002. "Forming a Spirituality of Wisdom." Pages 154-166 in *In Search of Wisdom: Faith Formation in the Black Church*. Edited by Anne Streaty Wimberly et al. Nashville: Abingdon Press.

Jensen, Eric. 1998. *Teaching with the Brain in Mind*. Alexandria, VA: Association for Supervision and Curriculum Development.

Johnson, Kent L. and Nelson T. Strobert. 1997. "Principles of Adult Learning." Pages 58-87 in *Lifelong Learning*. Edited by Rebecca Grothe. Minneapolis: Augsburg Fortress.

Larsen, Jerry Larsen. 2000. *Religious Education and the Brain*. New York: Paulist Press.

Lienhard, Marc. 1997. *La Foi Vecue*. Strasbourg, France: Faculte de Theologie Protestante.

Luther, Martin. 1529. "The Large Catechism." Pages 377-480 in *The Book of Concord: The Confessions of the Evangelical Lutheran Church*. Edited by Robert Kolb and Timothy J. Wengert. Minneapolis: Fortress Press, 2000.

McKenzie, Leon. 1985. "Developmental Spirituality and the Religious Educator." Pages 43-65 in *TheSpirituality of the Religious Educator*. Edited by James Michael Lee. Birmingham, Alabama: Religious Education Press.

Paris, Peter. 1995. *The Spirituality of African Peoples*. Minneapolis: Fortress Press.

Sigel, Irving E. and Rodney R. Cocking. 1977. *Cognitive Development from Childhood to Adolescence: A Constructivist Perspective*. New York: Holt, Rinehart and Winston.

Westerhoff, John. 1994. *Spiritual Life: the Foundation for Teaching and Preaching*. Louisville: Westminster John Knox Press.

Administrative Leadership as a Calling of the Spirit

Michael L. Cooper-White

Nearly three decades ago, upon graduation from the institution I now serve as president, I expected that my entire vocational life would be spent in parish ministry. After less than five years as a congregational pastor, however, a call came to serve in what has often been called "general church work." In accepting that call, I assured my parishioners and colleagues that it would be a brief detour on a side road, after which I would return to the parish thoroughfare where all true ministers travel. However, as Robert Frost put it in "The Road Less Traveled," way leads unto way, and some twenty years later I find myself still on the non-parochial road of ministerial leadership.

Along the journey, there have been more than a few cryptic comments and questions suggesting that I have abandoned real ministry and settled into the something less that is sometimes described almost with a slur: administration. "I could never be a paper pusher." "How can you stand all those meetings?" "You say you're a preacher, but you don't have a church?"

If my observations are correct, not only is there a measure of ambivalence in many circles regarding those who serve in non-parochial work, but many colleagues who serve in parish settings feel they are engaged in real ministry as long as they are doing anything but administrative work, however it may be defined. On the ministerial profiles of clergy seeking a call or appointment, administration is usually ranked near the bottom among multiple indicators of interest and competence. Interestingly enough, in my rounds of parish visits and my conversations with lay leaders, the question most frequently asked about seminaries is, "why aren't you teaching more about practical administration?" Parishioners seem to notice when their pastor is ambivalent about or ineffective in carrying out necessary administrative tasks that support and undergird the community's life under the Gospel. Of course, some also hold unrealistic views about the pastor's role, expecting her or him to be responsible for everything that goes on in the congregation.

Most people who offer themselves for church vocations have a deep sense that God has laid claim on their lives, that they want to walk closely with God, and be a leader among God's people. Whether the precise words are used or not, those so inclined express a sense of being called to a life of the Spirit, and of embracing a spiritual line of work. But many if not most, either by personal inclination or early indoctrination, become convinced that there are clearly demarcated arenas in which their spiritual calling will be exercised. "When I am preaching a sermon and leading worship, praying with a parishioner or counseling a lonely stranger, teaching the Bible, or visiting in people's homes or hospitals, then I am doing my true spiritual work. But when I am doing administrative tasks, that's a necessary evil or at least something that simply has to be done in support of the higher spiritual aspects of my calling."

One could speculate on why there is such widespread ambivalence and occasional outright hostility in church circles toward administrative leadership. For some, administrators are viewed as hierarchical autocrats or bureaucrats (the latter in Latin meaning literally "one who rules from a desk"). Some may have received unfair or even abusive treatment at the hands of an administrator, in school, the church or in a work setting. In an address delivered some years ago to the board of Augsburg/Fortress Publishers, William Lazareth pointed toward another dynamic that may be a cause of antipathy toward administrative work. Lazareth spoke of a widespread "organizational Pietism" which "is the simplistic and naive view that 'mission' is of God and administration is of Satan, and never the twain shall meet in this institutional church. Here, our Lord's counsel, 'Do not worry about tomorrow' (Matt 6:34) allegedly forbids all responsible planning" (Lazareth 1994).

In this chapter, my intent is to encourage readers to ponder anew some biblical, theological and practical considerations regarding administrative leadership, whether in ecclesiastical or secular settings. We begin by reflecting upon some perspectives from both the Old and New Testaments.

Administration as Creative Organizing, Naming, and Liberating

Two framed certificates sit atop a bookcase opposite the desk. On the left is a certificate of ordination; to the right is a Letter of Call to a post entitled president, by anyone's definition an administrative position. The first paragraph in the Letter of Call begins, "You are called to exercise this office as an ordained minister of Word and Sacrament, in mutual commitment with the people of this church for the sake of our mission and ministry in Christ's name."

By what authority does the Church call an individual to the work of administrative leadership? In the first place, it is with the encouragement of Holy Scripture. To see that this is so may require a degree of exegetical openness and imagination that escapes more traditional reading of the Bible. Searching "behind the text" and applying some good common sense will help in the exegetical process.

In the beginning, when God created the heavens and the earth, the earth was a formless void and darkness covered the face of the deep, while a wind from God swept over the face of the waters. Then God said, "Let there be light;" and there was light (Gen 1:1-3).

The divine act of creation itself—bringing order out of chaos—can be seen as the first administrative task. Through the power of the Divine Word, the Creator began to organize, to carry out a cosmic strategic plan, and to provide resources to enable the fulfillment of a grand vision. Out of *tohu va-vohu* God designed a structure, established orderly processes, and fostered an environment wherein all the subsequently created ones could live in harmony and fulfill their mission to be fruitful and to enjoy an abundant life.

> So out of the ground the Lord God formed every animal of the field and every bird of the air, and brought them to the man to see what he would call them; and whatever the man called every living creature, that was its name. (Gen 2:19).

In the divine call to name the other creatures, Adam was given the first human administrative responsibility. Name-giving in the ancient Near East was far more than a linguistic activity; it was an "exercise of sovereignty" (von Rad 1972, 83), a call to steward the well-being of other creatures. The created human one was to choreograph the dance of the other creatures, to listen carefully to each of their individual voices, and conduct them in a harmonious chorus that would glorify the Creator.

Further along in the Pentateuchal narrative, Moses, the one regarded by many as its central figure, must have been an effective administrative leader. Guiding a band of even several hundred former slaves on an extended wilderness expedition required some good planning and organizing (See Cooper-White, 2003, 40-41). Moses' self-effacing, liberating administrative style stands in dramatic counterpoint to that of Pharaoh's arrogant oppression.

> But Moses said to the Lord, "O my Lord, I have never been eloquent, neither in the past nor even now that you have spoken to your servant; but I am slow of speech and slow of tongue" (Exod 4:10).

Moses' assumption of the call to leadership came only after a period of divine coaxing, and perhaps some human coaching by his brother Aaron and others who recognized his potential. Once he accepted his call, however, Moses dedicated himself completely to the long-term challenge of stewarding a community, not for personal gain, but for the community's well-being and liberation.

Many other Old Testament stories could likewise be examined through the lens of how God was guiding and tending the people of Israel by means of inspiring and supporting gifted administrative leaders like Abraham and Sarah, Isaac and Rebekah, Jacob and Rachel, Joshua, Joseph and others.

Administration as Guiding the Ship of Faith

In the New Testament, particularly in the book of Acts and the Pauline epistles, there are explicit references to the calling of administration. In Paul's great chapter on Christian vocation, the apostle includes administration among the divinely appointed spiritual gifts (1 Cor 12:28). The Greek word commonly rendered "administration," *kubernesis*, literally means "steermanship" or being a helmsman (Mitchell 1991, 163). Keeping the ship afloat, piloting it through both calm and turbulent seas, coordinating the work of the crew, calming the passengers, making frequent adjustments amidst constantly changing environmental conditions, all the while pressing on toward the destination, is the helmsman's challenge.

Regarding Paul's inclusion of *kubernesis* among the spiritual gifts entrusted to the Christian community, Hermann Wolfgang Beyer notes:

The reference can only be to the specific gifts which qualify a Christian to be a helmsman to his [*sic*] congregation, i.e., a true director of its order and therewith of its life. What was the scope of this directive activity in the time of Paul we do not know. This was a period of fluid development. The importance of the helmsman increases in a time of storm. The office of directing the congregation may well have developed especially in emergencies both within and without. The proclamation of the Word was not originally one of its tasks (Beyer 1966, 1036).

Beyer points to the outpouring of Christian artistic expressions which portray Jesus at the helm of a ship tossed about on a stormy sea. This artistic tradition, coupled with the New Testament texts, suggests that administrative service as a steer-person or helmsman is always an act of stewardship, i.e., that those engaged in administrative leadership of a community are accountable to the One who finally charts the course and determines the destination.

Leadership as Vocation:
Theological and Confessional Affirmations

In addition to the Bible, a second source of authority by which the Church has deemed it appropriate to call some individuals to posts with a heavily administrative leaning is our theological tradition. The assertion *finitum capax infiniti* (the finite is capable of the infinite), suggests that within mundane administrative human activity one may encounter God's revelation and experience God's love. That which is infinite, indescribable, incapable of adequate rational explanation, i.e., spiritual, is not confined by human preconceptions and should not be limited by our propensities to limit the arenas in which the Spirit may be at work. Martin Luther's many comments about the vocational holiness of mundane tasks flows from his incarnational conviction that God is "deep in the flesh." In this regard, routine administrative tasks may be as spiritual or holy as the functions fulfilled by a priest in the sanctuary. A congregational treasurer working in the wee hours to balance the books may be as much engaged in a spiritual endeavor as a pastor praying on her or his *prie-dieu*.

For many in our day, the epitome of what it means to be an administrator might be found in the legal profession. Over against all the disparaging lawyer jokes stands Luther's strong conviction that officers of the court serve in a holy calling:

> Just as a pious theologian and sincere preacher is called, in the realm of Christ, an angel of God, a savior, prophet, priest, servant, and teacher, so a pious jurist and true scholar can be called, in the worldly realm of the emperor, a prophet, priest, angel, and savior. . . . When I speak of the jurists, I do not mean only the Doctors of Laws, but the whole profession, including chancellors, secretaries, judges, advocates, notaries, and all who have to do with the legal side of government (LW 46:239-240).

This theological understanding of vocation is clearly articulated by the Lutheran Confessions. The Augsburg Confession recognizes the divine ordering of the universe and the importance of human processes and procedures to maintain good order in both ecclesiastical and civil arenas. In encouraging Christians to hold public office, and to serve as judges and princes, the confessions affirmed the nature of ecclesiastical administration and governmental service as callings of the Spirit (CA XIV, XVI, XXVII). In the key article defining the Church, the true *ecclesia* is deemed to exist where the Word of God is preached and the holy sacraments are administered according to the Gospel (CA VII). Thus, an act of administration—of careful, hospitable table-setting and preparing the holy meal for the faithful—is constitutive and foundational for the Church, not something peripheral.

Spirit-led Leadership as a Communal Endeavor

In her article, "Leadership from a Feminist Perspective," Lynn Rhodes points to the importance of seeing ministry as a communal activity:

> The work of ministry is the work of empowerment and social transformation of communities. Leadership in that kind of work needs to learn how to function collaboratively. . . .We will need to develop a spirituality that is rooted in the welfare of the community. Much of what we are seeing today is an individualized spirituality that is cut off from connection (Rhodes 1993, 17).

For Lutherans, the office of ministry is divinely appointed, instituted by God for the sake of tending the Gospel in a particular community of God's faithful people. Ministry, therefore, is inherently public. The pastoral office belongs to the community, both the gathered congregation and the wider expression of the one, holy, catholic and apostolic church. Thus, in our tradition, an individual's sense of being called by God must be confirmed by the church, the community.

In declaring that public ministry is an inherently communal affair, not an individual's prerogative or free agency, the Augsburg Confession states that "nobody should publicly teach or preach or administer the sacraments in the church without a regular call" (CA XIV). That is, one does not set up shop as a minister by personal whim or by virtue of a pious feeling of having been called by God. Rather, the church as a community of believers invites, prepares, nurtures and grants authority for an individual to carry out its public ministry. That this ministry is broadly public is signaled in the current practice of the Evangelical Lutheran Church in America whereby a congregation's call must also be "attested" and signed by a bishop. One is called not just to serve a local community, but to engage collegially in a broader communal public ministry.

Whether or not one is on a roster of ordained or lay ministers set apart by a church body, an administrative calling must be exercised within this broad understanding of the communal nature of ministry. What might this mean in actual day to day practice? Among other things, it points toward an attitude of seeing oneself as servant of the community's visions and values, as engaged in carrying out the collective mission that sometimes diverges from one's own perspectives and priorities. Reflecting on the importance of constantly upholding a communal vision as one engages in administrative leadership, Donald Senior writes:

> Those in administrative leadership have to care for the institution as a whole, not just one part of it. . . .The work of the administrator is plunged into the public and communal dimensions of an institution, having to interact with all the groups and interests that make it up. Surely, having to work with the community of people that forms an institution, people in all their glory and their shame, involves us in something that is close to the heart of the gospel (Senior 1999, 4).

To be engaged in leading and facilitating the work of a community means that an administrator is intrinsically involved in a political process. The very word "political" is taboo in most church circles, and many folks become disillusioned and walk away sadly shaking their heads when they discover "there's politics even in the church." But to be a people, a *polis*, engaged in God's mission (i.e. to be the *ekklesia*) means that the process whereby a community comes together, shapes a mission and negotiates the many necessary compromises—small and sometimes larger—by which individual desires are blended into a cohesive holistic movement, is a political process. A challenge for an administrator—literally "one who ministers to" (from Latin *ad ministrare*)—is to prayerfully tend the political process so that God's salvific mission is indeed fulfilled. Additionally, the tender of the process should give attention to the well-being of individuals, seeing to it that the political process builds up each person and enables her or his gifts to flourish in service to God and the greater *polis*.

Good stewardship of the communal aspect of administrative work includes the recognition that there are limits to a collaborative style. Even the most collegial leader will face occasions when s/he has to make a final decision; avoiding doing so can inhibit the work of others or even paralyze an entire community.

Eric Gritsch reflects on how "the communion of believers exists in space and time as a visible sign of our future with God through Christ" (Gritsch 1994, 113). Noting that a popular motif among Christians as they reflect on ministry is "servanthood," Gritsch asserts that balancing it should be an appropriate measure of "serpenthood."

> The serpent is the symbol of medicine; surgery is the exercising of tough love on the physical body. In hospital trauma stations and emergency rooms, one does what is necessary to save a life, according to hard and consistent lifesaving training, and without asking for a vote among the patient and the patient's family as to procedure. Human reason is the basis of this kind of love (Gritsch 1994, 113).

In the constant interplay of servanthood and serpenthood, an administrative leader may strive to be a facilitator of communal activity and shared decision-making. But on occasion, for the sake of the community's well-being, the leader must exercise rational, cold-blooded decision-making that will not please all or even a majority of its members.

A Spiritual Pathway: Some Practical Possibilities

In recent years, there has emerged a substantial collection of books and articles on "leadership" written by authors from the arenas of business, education, the military, and non-profit organizations. Almost all cite examples and case studies of both good and ineffective leaders; most also set forth a list of key traits and habits of strong, effective administrators who get things done and propel their organizations to new levels of success. Many of these writings, even from so-called secular authors and arenas, speak of spiritual dimensions of leadership.

But rarely do these popular works probe the profound theological questions of vocation. What is God's mission in this time and place, and what is my/our part in the divine mission? If the key to any administrator's job description is getting things done, what is it that God wants to be done? And likewise, if the way things are done may be as important as ultimate outcomes or products, how might an administrative leader conduct her/himself so as to enable a community's spiritual gifts to flourish?

In his pioneering work on Lutheran spirituality, Bradley Hanson defines spirituality as "a faith plus a path." Spirituality, says Hanson, "is a living faith that is nurtured and expressed by certain practices that together make up a spiritual path" (Hanson 2000, 146). While each individual engaged in the vocation of administration will have her/his own unique ways of working, are there some signposts or markers that may help keep one's journey on a Spirit-led pathway? A few such possible markers are offered below, inviting the reader to expand and develop her/his own list of spiritual guideposts.

Prayerful Posture: A Spirit-centered approach to leadership surely must mean more than simply offering a perfunctory prayer at the beginning of every meeting. In many if not almost all so-called secular arenas, doing so would be inappropriate, coercive and perhaps even illegal. But approaching tasks and decisions from a prayerful posture may well be at the heart of the matter of what it means to be a spiritually-attuned person engaged in an administrative calling. If one aspires to be an administrator who is led by the Spirit, then nurturing a vibrant personal and communal prayer life is important.

Telling Titles: Creating trite catch phrases, or misappropriating ecclesiastical terminology can be manipulative and an empty exercise. Nevertheless, there is value in giving careful attention as job titles and position descriptions are created. For example, in our seminary we no longer have a person with the common title of development director. Instead, our lead resource developer is called the Vice President for Stewardship and Leadership Development. In the end, her work is simply about engaging in prayerful conversation with individuals, groups and churches regarding their exercise of Christian stewardship. Likewise, rather than directors of admission, we have two Associate Deans for Church Vocations. Their ultimate goal is not to admit students to Gettysburg Seminary, but rather to help individuals discern their vocational calling.

Self-identity Sustainers: Lutherans, late-comers to contemporary conversations about "spirituality," are learning much from other traditions. In the Episcopal Church, all non-parochial clergy are expected to be "attached to an altar." This means that a priest employed in a non-parochial setting normally is assigned by her/his bishop to a parish for regular Sunday duties. Often this service is on a non-stipendiary basis so that such non-parish priests' gifts may be deployed in congregations with limited resources. In the frequent exercise of one's clerical identity by preaching, teaching, presiding at the sacraments or extending pastoral care, the priest or pastor is reminded of her/his fundamental vocational calling.

Collegial Connections: A common theme running through writings about Christian spirituality is that its practice involves a lifestyle rhythm which vacillates frequently between solitude and life in community. For those of us whose callings carry within them a heavy administrative component, establishing and maintaining collegial connections is critical. While spending time alone in reflection and prayer is important for any leader, so is being in the company of sisters and brothers who are fellow travelers in similar circles. Peer groups and professional associations can be the lifeblood in nurturing one's spirituality as an administrator. Seeking mentors and mentoring others ought to be an intentional lifelong discipline for those called to ministries of administrative leadership.

Expansive Empowering: The commitment to engage in constant and ever-widening collegial connectivity flows from some basic core theological convictions. Key among them is a theology of abundance in the face of our society's unrelenting reinforcement of a competitive philosophy of scarcity. At the heart of this dichotomy is an understanding of the nature of power. If power is a limited quantity, then my having more means that you will have less. If, on the other hand, we can empower one another, i.e., if interpersonal and relational power is unlimited and can be ever expanding, sharing my knowledge will not only empower you but will expand my influence as well. Recent publications by feminist authors are particularly helpful in exploring further this discussion of what Pamela Cooper-White refers to as "power-in-community" (Cooper-White 1995, 38ff).

Transformative Transparency: It has been said that "democracies die behind closed doors." So does the long-term effectiveness of administrators who tend to horde power, or keep insights and information close to the vest lest competitors get a leg up by virtue of employing this shared information in their own organizations. A high level of transparency in communication—sharing information broadly, openly communicating rationales for decisions—tends to promote health and can be truly transformative, especially in troubled organizations. One of the tell-tale signs of an unhealthy or dysfunctional community is the existence of a host of family secrets that are known by only a few. Of course, nothing said here is to suggest that an administrator should be cavalier or other than entirely scrupulous in keeping confidences, respecting the privacy of personnel matters and otherwise maintaining appropriate boundaries in the stewarding of information.

Spirituality Shaped by Social Location

A collegial group of great value in my current calling is the conference of presidents of the eight Evangelical Lutheran Church in America seminaries. One of my mentors is the Rev. Dr. James Echols, who serves as president of the Lutheran School of Theology in Chicago. In our gatherings, President Echols frequently reminds us of the importance of recognizing how one's social location determines in great measure how s/he sees the world. Social location is determined by many factors—gender, ethnicity, economic status, primary language, and educational background, among others.

Not only are one's perspectives and judgments influenced by "where I stand" in the global community, but so is an individual's spiritual journey influenced by paths both trodden and not taken. In contemplating various expressions of spirituality and how those expressions get lived out in administrative leadership or other callings, therefore, one does well to be somewhat tentative and non-prescriptive. Because we start from different social locations, and because our envisioned destinations may differ considerably, our spiritual pathways may twist and turn in quite distinctive directions.

In terms of nurturing and expressing one's Christian spirituality while serving in various forms of administrative leadership, therefore, each individual has to discern her/his own way of responding to the Spirit's calling. So, too, in today's increasingly diverse and multicultural context, one may be called to exercise leadership within a community where there are sharply differing notions of what "spiritual leadership" might look like. To steward authority wisely and exercise leadership appropriately in these times requires great sensitivity, careful listening to multiple constituencies, and an openness to recognize and believe that the Spirit may truly be doing a new thing!

In addition to cultural, economic, educational and other dimensions, one's current social location is also defined by length of service in a particular context. Those who remain in leadership posts long-term comment on the importance of recognizing that an organization or institution is constantly changing, as is the context or environment in which one's ministry is carried out. Every so often, accordingly, an administrative leader asks her/himself and reflects with at least a few trusted advisers upon questions such as: Am I still the leader this organization needs for the next chapter of its life? Am I continuing to grow spiritually in this calling? Are God and this community of God's people still calling me to be here? In his autobiographical reflections on this matter, Kurt Senske writes:

> Admittedly, the process one goes through to answer these questions is often gut-twisting and soul-wrenching. It requires a willingness to engage in painful self-examination and to get second opinions from friends, enemies, coaches, colleagues, and spouses. It requires putting others' interests ahead of one's own (Senske 2003, 27).

Lyle Schaller's reflections on assessing chapters of ministry in a parish setting merit consideration in pondering one's administrative leadership in other settings as well (See Schaller 1977). Schaller suggests that in collegial reflection, looking back over ministry in a particular setting, one can begin to identify chapters the beginnings and endings of which are marked by significant events, crises, accomplishments or developmental tasks. Each chapter may place its own unique demands upon various leaders. At some point, Schaller suggests, a spiritual leader may determine that s/he no longer has the gifts needed for the next chapter, or is simply ready for a new challenge in a new setting. Among colleague seminary presidents who are "long in the tooth" in this work, I have heard comments that in order to remain effective and spiritually alive, they have had to reinvent their own leadership style several times.

Because any leader's perspectives are inherently shaped and limited by her/his social location, those who embrace administrative callings in our time need to strive constantly to see the bigger picture, to travel in ever-widening circles even as they mind the store and tend to the daily details in their own organizations. The insights from what is often called "systems thinking" have been found valuable by many leaders. Often, the solution to a problem is found by looking over the hedgerow into a neighbor's backyard, by thinking "outside the box" just slightly, by recognizing that the context in which we function is a bit larger than it appears.

Delivering the commencement address at his alma mater 50 years ago, Stewart Herman echoed themes sounded previously by John Wesley. Herman, whose own career included pastoring in Germany during the rise of Nazism, international refugee and disaster relief work, and service in the U.S. Office of Special Services (OSS, precursor to the CIA), understood what it means to pursue a spiritual pathway through the thickets of political complexity in a sinful world. In his comments to the Gettysburg Seminary graduating class of 1954, Herman urged the newly-minted theologs to think broadly and stretch themselves spiritually by seeking to break out of their own limited social locations:

Today the very nature of the non-Christian world in which we live charges us as ministers of Christ not only with the cure of souls but with the care of all the churches. These two things go together. I charge you as priests and prophets of the church to concentrate upon your parish as thought it were the world, and to concentrate upon the world as though it were your parish (Herman 1954).

Administrative Leadership as Spiritual Syzygy

In his sermon at the service of my installation as director of an urban coalition of parishes, Bishop Stanley Olson of the former Lutheran Church in America's Pacific Southwest Synod encouraged me to be like Syzygus, an obscure figure mentioned only once in the Bible (Phil 4:3). Syzygus is translated into English as "true yokefellow" or "loyal companion." That self-image as one engaged in spiritual syzygy or connecting and fellow-traveling has stuck with me through the series of my subsequent calls in the church. In each place of service, including its administrative dimensions, I have attempted to be a connector, one who helps people build bridges to one another, and a fellow traveler amidst a community on a spiritual journey.

In conclusion, it is my conviction that the work of administrative leadership—whether in churchly or secular settings—is a holy calling. In the daily tasks of attending or conducting meetings, dealing with mountains of paperwork, issuing memoranda and responding to emails by the dozens or hundreds, an administrator with eyes to see and ears to hear will catch occasional visions of the face, and hear at least faint echoes of the voice of God. In tending, nourishing and sometimes healing the connective tissues that bind together an organization, however large or small, a spiritually attuned administrator is an agent of the Holy One, engaged in strengthening the Body of Christ.

References

Cooper-White, Michael L. 2003. *On a Wing and a Prayer: Faithful Leadership in the 21st Century.* Minneapolis: Augsburg Fortress.

Cooper-White, Pamela. 1995. *The Cry of Tamar.* Minneapolis: Augsburg Fortress.

Gritsch, Eric W. 1994. *Fortress Introduction to Lutheranism.* Minneapolis: Fortress Press.

Hanson, Bradley. 2000. *A Graceful Life: Lutheran Spirituality for Today.* Minneapolis: Augsburg Books.

Herman, Stewart. 1954. "Commencement Address 1954." Lutheran Theological Seminary at Gettysburg: Library Collection.

Beyer, Hermann Wolfgang. 1965. "Kubernesis." Pages 1035-1037 in *Theological Dictionary of the New Testament.* Volume 3. Edited by Gerhard Kittel. Translated and edited by Geoffrey W. Bromiley. Grand Rapids, Mich: Wm—Eerdmans Publishing Company.

Kolb, Robert and Timothy J. Wengert, eds. 2000. *The Book of Concord: The Confessions of the Evangelical Lutheran Church.* Translated by Charles Arand, et al. Minneapolis: Fortress Press.

Lazareth, William H. 1994. "Theology and Administration of the ELCA Publishing House, Augsburg/Fortress." Unpublished paper.

Luther, Martin. 1530. "A Sermon on Keeping Children in School." Pages 213-258 in *Luther's Works*, vol 44. Edited by Robert C. Schultz. Philadelphia: Fortress Press, 1967.

Mitchell, Margaret M. 1991. *Paul and the Rhetoric of Reconciliation*. Louisville: Westminster/John Knox Press.

Rhodes, Lynn N. 1993. "Leadership from a Feminist Perspective." *Word and World* 13/1:13-18.

Schaller, Lyle. 1977. *Survival Tactics in the Parish*. Nashville: Abingdon.

Senior, Donald. 1999. "The Gospel at the Heart of Our Work: Biblical Reflections on Administrative Service." *In Trust* New Year:4-6

Senske, Kurt. 2003. *Executive Values: A Christian Approach to Organizational Leadership*. Minneapolis: Augsburg Books.

Von Rad, Gerhard. 1972. *Genesis*. Revised edition. Old Testament Library. Translated by John H. Marks. Philadelphia: The Westminster Press.

Teaching Spirituality with Luther and Medieval Women Mystics

Kirsi Stjerna

In a course on the Lutheran Confessions, after studying all of the marvelous things that Luther has to say about spiritual living in his Catechisms, a student asked: "how come we do not do any of that in our seminary?" This question, reflecting the feeling of many entering the seminary, contains a particular yet fuzzy notion of what spirituality is and what role it should play in theological education.

In this brief essay I will reflect on my experiences of teaching "spirituality-related" courses in a seminary setting and how I see teaching spirituality the "Lutheran way" to have many possibilities. I approach the subject as a historian with my left foot in theology.

Seminarians have an exciting opportunity to explore the great writers of Christian history, writers who articulated the basics and different nuances of Christian faith through their personal voices. From these writings students gain an appreciation of what Christian theology holds, what gives meaning for the various practices and institutions in the church, and, in general, what Christianity is about and what keeps it alive. Study of the history of the development of Christian faith and practice, as well as the study of the core beliefs and their different interpretations, is ultimately always about spirituality, even if students, or teachers, are not always aware of or explicit about it.

It is not unusual to hear a first-year student complain after the first semester, that Early Church History, Pentateuch, and Preaching "are all so academic," expressing yearning for something "more spiritual." Behind such puzzlement and dissatisfaction often lies a particular but limited view of spirituality and of what theological training should be. People easily associate the word spirituality with devotional practices, without realizing that that is only one aspect of spirituality.

It is of interest that in some other languages the word equivalent to spirituality sounds broader and more inclusive, while being more specific about what is meant. For instance, "Geistlichkeit" in German, and "hengellisyys" in Finnish. A common denominator in these words is the noun Spirit, "Geist" and "henki"; they both refer to teachings and practices that have to do with life with the Spirit and in the Spirit, that is, godly life, religious life that is oriented by belief in the Divine Spirit and how that touches human life. Thus the broad-sounding word is actually understood quite specifically. Internationally, the word can be understood as referring to all those things that have to do with the personal dimension of one's religiosity and awareness of God's Spirit working in one's life. The word is not limited to the personal aspect but has an outward tendency as it shapes a person's life and actions, and is sustained and expressed in an institutional way in a church that operates in the world. Also, theologically speaking, the focus of spirituality is outside oneself, in the Spirit who "creates" spiritual being and living, in other words, spirituality. In some languages the word for spirituality refers to particularly Christian religiosity, to religious life sustained by the Spirit of the God worshipped by Christians. In the American context the word spirituality is used in many different ways than is the case in some other languages. In American usage the word spirituality has lost its primarily Christian connotation. It does not necessarily refer to the beliefs and practices around the Spirit of the Triune God. The same is not true, for instance, in Finnish, where the word for spirituality, "hengellisyys," refers to a particular Christian experience, faith, and practice—whereas another word, "uskonnollisuus," religiosity, refers to the multiplicity of religious experiences, beliefs and rituals.

This is to say that the word spirituality is widely used but often times in quite confusing and differing ways. There seems to be somewhat limited assumptions of what Christian spirituality is as a form of personal practice and intentional living, while the word spirituality in its wider use remains ambiguous and without a definition. At the same time, there is a great interest in spirituality of all kinds.

One particular school year, with a large class of students having survived their first academic semester, quite a few of them wanted to do something "spiritual," to "feel connected again," to be reminded again of the reasons of why they had entered the seminary. With these yearnings, a number of students enrolled in a course on Medieval Women as Spiritual Teachers. Some expected a week-long course centered on devotional reading and practice and were surprised to be asked to learn the history of particular women writers, to understand these women's contexts and the problems they faced when developing and using their voice as spiritual teachers, to examine their writings and theology—and while doing all that, learn about the role of gender (and the dominance of the male experience and views) in Christian history and spirituality. As a result, though, the class in general expressed satisfaction for what the readings and writers and intense encounter with them managed to give them "spiritually," namely, important connections with the past practitioners of faith, affirmation of one's own historical identity in the process of discerning which stories one can hold as one's own and which not, several moments of "aha" and "me too"—as well as "not me"—and a deepened awareness of the precious continuity of Christian faith and the timelessness of ultimate concerns: finding meaning, rooted-ness, and direction; finding God and a godly direction and meaning in one's life. Through academic historical and theological study, medieval women became spiritual teachers for modern-day Protestant seminarians.

How, why? That remains a mystery, but I believe it has to do with the materials that deal with "ultimate concerns," connecting and conversing with other people, dead or alive, pondering and living through existential questions and situations, similar or different. History itself gives individuals identity and a sense of continuity and transported meaning, it allows one to define oneself through stories with which one connects. Particularly when one adds the God-dimension to the examination of stories and experiences of dealing with the "meaning" question, study of history can be a profoundly spiritual exercise.

"Spirituality" courses do not have to be offered as such in order for students of theology to be able to connect the academic, the personal, and the spiritual. History, in particular, is an extremely fruitful discipline in this regard. I would argue that the study of spirituality and its practices is impossible without a sense of history. Conversely, when one talks about human history, one can hardly do that without appreciating the role of human beings' spiritual concerns and intentions.

As this book argues, and as I argue, the teaching and studying of spirituality in a seminary setting happens in direct and indirect ways, through academic work, practical experiences, devotional exercises, worship, personal interaction in and out of the classroom—a mix of influences and information that in the end will provide students with the ingredients sufficient to bake a cake that does not collapse. The goal is to teach and preach and practice and live spirituality that is rooted in history, sound in theology, and expressed in communal faith and faith-practices that rest on the solid ground of a tested and shared faith, without demanding that others "be alike" but fostering spirituality that appreciates the diversity and many dimensions of spirituality itself, which by nature cannot be too rigid.

I have found teaching the Christian mystics, such as medieval women visionary writers, to be a very effective tool in exploring the world of spirituality theologically, historically and personally with my students. Needless to say, study in a Lutheran setting of medieval catholic women with universally pertinent faith issues lends an automatic ecumenical lens to further study of theology and spirituality.

To be more specific, some of the medieval women are easier to learn "from" as spiritual teachers and inspirations than others. For instance, St. Teresa of Avila succeeded in implementing a vision for reform of her order based on her timelessly relevant model of prayer. She was so successful that she is widely recognized as one of the most significant spiritual teachers and religious leaders in the history of Christianity. Her life story, her drivenness, her visionary ways, as well as her theological reflection and model for spiritual living offer connecting points for students today who are looking for further understanding of their faith, their tradition, and their call as teachers and leaders. Another example of a timeless teacher is Dame Julian from Norwich, a theologian whose reflections on God and suffering and the non-existence of evil in the divine realm continue to inspire readers who are trying to reconcile their theology of the goodness of the creator and the manifest suffering in the world. Hildegard of Bingen and Birgitta of Sweden set models for action and contemplation, spirituality that enables a person to be engaged with the world and issues in society. They model how religion, science and politics are intertwined, and thus present a holistic approach to life and offer valuable spiritual insights.

Even those women whose struggles with their humanness in the face of dualistic body/spirit ideals of the time and whose self-humiliating, often cruel, spiritual habits appear strange to us—such as Marie d'Oignes and Catherine of Genoa, known for their outrageous acts of self-humiliation and self-inflicted pain—can serve as teachers with their testimonies of the power of religious experience, passion for their cause, and the intensity with which they approached life and expressed their spirituality.[27]

Studying medieval women reminds modern readers of the mystical aspect of spirituality, of the power of a meaningful experience and the importance of spiritual habits that nurture theological reflection and action in the midst of daily life. Almost without exception they present a model of spirituality that is personally transformative and that provides the impetus to be active in the world in service of God and the other.

Most importantly, in my view, the mystics teach us about humility in the face of God and godly issues, they teach us of the importance of passion and intentionality in God-relationship, of the nobility of a deliberate search for deeper knowledge of oneself, one's neighbor and God, of the limits of human knowledge, experience and language when it comes to God, and of the importance of giving oneself to others as God has given godself to us. They model spirituality and spiritual living as something that encompasses both internal and external; for them spirituality and spiritual living are about a transformation that happens in personal, mystical encounter with God and how that relationship with the Divine gives the person an identity and a call in one's place, that is, it directs and motivates one's purposeful, meaningful living, life with a godly meaning.

Medieval women as a group of teachers teach about the significance of intentionality and habit in fostering spiritual life, and they demonstrate as well the vital intersection between faith and one's actions. Their teaching power rests on the continuity of ultimate concerns, the basic questions human beings deal with: who am I, who is God, how do we connect, what is God's meaning in my life, where do I find solace, comfort and direction. These are timelessly valid questions, and inspiring insights around them can be gathered from the varied stories and voices of the mystics.[28]

What often strikes as alien to Lutherans is the medieval women's experience of or yearning for mystical union with God, together with the use of mystical language when referring to experiences of a supernatural nature—experiences that cannot be evaluated from the outside, for which there is no rational, scientific explanation, but which have a profound meaning for the person involved as well for the people around her or him.

Studying the women also brings up the relevance of gender. Namely, spiritual practices and teachings have differed and have been experienced and expressed differently due to gender differences or gender restrictions. Instead of enforcing further dichotomies, this awareness adds to the appreciation of the different dimensions and faces of spirituality. I would hesitate to use labels such as "feminine" and "masculine" spirituality, but we can certainly recognize certain elements and traits in spirituality expressed by women. The reasons for these differences lie not necessarily in differences between the two sexes but in the societal constructions around gender which limited and guided women's options in spiritual living and expression.[29] Study of women and men and their spiritual lives and teachings allows us to see the complexity of spirituality as such and how so many factors, such as gendered context, play a role in the shape and language of one's spirituality.

Now I want to turn to Luther and argue for what makes Luther a timeless and potentially ecumenical spiritual teacher.

Luther has been one of the most powerful Christian teachers with a unique vision of what life with God is and can be about in the world. His teachings in their entirety are about that, spiritual teachings around different theological and practical topics, which often include practical advice about "how to go about it." His theology is not only about doctrine but arises from his own wrestling, from experiences of despair and joy with God, and from his constant, diligent reading of the Bible. To him theology is a matter or life and death. If he had used the word spirituality, he would have regarded it as a matter of life and death as well. To Luther life and thought, practice and theory, doctrine of God and human life with God belong together. One way to keep them together is through spiritual theology—with theology that is never far apart from real life issues and situations and that is shaped by real life experiences, and spirituality that draws from theology, understanding and experience of God that rests on biblical revelation and the reader's discovery of the meaning of revelation in his/her place.

In his Catechisms Luther offers a vision, or a model for a spirituality that is historical, theologically articulated, and supported by and lived out in particular religious practices, at home and in the worship community. He managed to phrase his vision of God's working for and in human life and giving human lives godly meaning in a way that is timelessly valuable (notwithstanding his patriarchal directives about the order of household and society, etc.), not only in his catechisms but also other treatises, sermons, and even hymns. Many of his texts can be taken as spiritual sources, exposition of a vision for spiritual living. In his catechisms, in particular, one can see this most clearly. In his explanation of the Ten Commandments he offers directives for daily life, in his exposition of the Lord's Prayer he teaches spiritual habits, and in his interpretation of the Creed he gives a theological foundation for individual and communal spiritual living, in a worship community and at home.[30] Needless to say, study of Luther's theology and selected treatises is thus always a spiritual exercise and an opportunity to think theologically about the foundations and manifestations of spiritual life rooted in theology. In Luther's theology, spirituality is never absent but always part of the whole. Luther does not compartmentalize spirituality. To him all aspects of life are about life with the Spirit. It is this premise in his inclusive vision of holiness which radically altered the exclusive medieval Christian notion of what is spiritual and what is not.

In Luther's theology, one finds a vision for spirituality that is inclusive, biblical and theological and historical, and existential. To him theology lives and is to be experienced in life, to him spirituality is about theology, that is, about God. This has to do with Luther's unique theology of the Word and, thereby, his understanding of God's presence and work as the Spirit through the Word.[31]

In my view, the very basis of Luther's theology is about how God works through God's Word in omnipresent and omnipowerful ways, in ways that we never fully understand. His trust in God's presence in human life is articulated in his theology of redemption and in his Christology, his theology of the cross. Especially clear in the Catechisms is his view on God's presence as the Spirit, a presence that embraces human life fully and transforms human life through mysterious yet concrete Divine acts.[32] Also his theology of grace versus works highlights the initiative of God and God's Spirit in "spiriting" human lives. He explains how "spirit-ual" is always about and of God. In explaining the Creed he states the basis for Lutheran spirituality: "I believe that by my own understanding or strength I cannot believe in Jesus Christ my Lord or come to him, but instead the Holy Spirit has called me through the gospel, enlightened me with his gifts, made me holy and kept me in the true faith, just as he calls, gathers, enlightens, and makes holy the whole Christian church. . . " (Kolb and Wengert 2000, 355).

Thus, judging from Luther's starting points and emphasis, spirituality depends on God in the same manner as the entire creation does. Central to Lutheran spirituality is the conviction of human beings becoming justified by grace by alien faith, with alien righteousness and thus becoming divine in personal relation with God the sanctifier.[33] Both teaching and practice in Lutheran spirituality rest on this principle. Luther's emphasis on proclaiming the Word and administering the sacraments speaks of trust in God's promise and action. His trust in the real effect of the sacraments is articulated clearly throughout his treatises and presents a unique expression of spirituality resting on God's promise, the Word, and acts performed based on the Word. One could say that behind his notion of faith and Word, both central for Lutheran spirituality, is a mystical dimension—the mysterious way in which God gives and comes to human beings, in faith, through the Word.[34]

In light of his catechisms, Luther's spirituality is based on the doctrine of a gracious God, the work of Christ and God's promise to do good things to us. His spirituality is concrete and personal. What God has promised comes to each of us via Word and the "tools" of grace. That this happens really and truly is a Lutheran conviction—and nowhere else manifest and confessed more than in baptismal and eucharistic practice.

These basic notions in Lutheran theology form the basis and vision for Lutheran spirituality that is inclusive, broad, and extroverted.

Luther's as well as the mystics' teachings encourage students of spirituality to stick with the Word, the texts, and to look for meanings for the people before them as well as for themselves. They inspire students to think of human lives and experiences theologically and to dare to include personal insights and experiences into theology. In so doing, they give students a model for spirituality. They also inspire students to look at the world with open eyes to see and experience God's presence in the most surprising places and moments, that is, in all of God's creation that has come about because of the act of God's Word. Learning from the intentional spiritual practice and passion of the mystics and from Luther's theological convictions about the word and his vision for spiritual habits in search of divine meaning, students of spirituality can endeavor to explicate and experience how, as the catechism phrases it, "this" could come "to us." "This" being spirituality and a sense of the Spirit's presence and work in one's own life. "This" can also be understood as the Word, as God present in human life through the Word. Both Luther and the mystics yearned for that experience, and wrote theologically about the meaning and premises of the encounter of God with human beings in the Word. They left us with their "word" about their encounter with the Word and the meaning they derived from that experience. With Luther we can ask, what does all this mean when it "comes to us"—"this" being the meaning of the Word.

References

Bynum, Caroline Walker. 1991. *Fragmentation and Redemption. Essays on Gender and the Human Body in Medieval Religion*. New York: Zone Books.

Hoffman, Bengt R. 1998. *Theology of the Heart: the Role of Mysticism in the Theology of Martin Luther*. Edited by Pearl Willemssen Hoffman. Minneapolis: Kirkhouse Press.

Kolb, Robert and Timothy J. Wengert, ed. 2000. *The Book of Concord: the Confessions of the Evangelical Lutheran Church*. Minneapolis: Fortress Press.

Stjerna, Kirsi. 2002. "Spiritual Models of Medieval Mystics Today: Rethinking the Legacy of Birgitta of Sweden." *Studies in Spirituality* 12:126-140.

Stjerna, Kirsi. 2001. "Stories of Medieval Women for Today." Pages 37-52 in *Women Christian Mystics Speak to Our Times*. Edited by David B. Perrin, O.M.I. Franklin, Wisconsin: Sheed & Ward.

Authors/Contributors

William O. Avery, D.Min. Lutheran Theological Seminary at Gettysburg
Professor of Field Education and the Arthur L. Larson Professor of
Stewardship and Parish Ministry

J. Paul Balas, Ph.D. The University of Pittsburgh
Professor Emeritus of Pastoral Theology

Gerald Christianson, Ph.D. The University of Chicago
Central Pennsylvania Synod Professor of Church History

Michael L. Cooper-White, D.D. Susquehanna University
President of the Seminary

Maria Erling, Th.D. Harvard Divinity School
Associate Professor of the History of Christianity in North America,
and Global Missions

Mark W. Oldenburg, Ph.D. Drew University
Professor of Liturgics

Brooks Schramm, Ph.D. The University of Chicago
Associate Professor of Biblical Studies

Robin J. Steinke, Ph.D. The University of Cambridge
Dean of the Seminary
Associate Professor of Ethics and Public Life

Kirsi Stjerna, Ph.D. Boston University
Associate Professor of Reformation Church History

Nelson T. Strobert, Ph.D. The University of Akron
Professor of Christian Education

Norma Schweitzer Wood, D.Min. The Catholic University of America
Professor Emeritus of Pastoral Counseling and Interpersonal
Ministries

Endnotes

Spirituality, Spiritual Formation, and Preparation for Pastoral Ministry

[1] The school was Theil College in Greenville, Pennsylvania, where I had the privilege of participating for four years in the Theil Choir under the direction of Marlowe W. Johnson.

Luther, Lutherans, and Spirituality

[2] This article is based on a paper originally presented at the annual meeting of the Society of Anglican and Lutheran Theologians in Nashville, November 2000. *Sewanee Theological Review* published a revised version of the paper in December 2002. A further revision is printed here, with the permission of *STR*. This paper does not attempt to be original analysis of Luther's texts but rather dialogue and assessment of Luther's thought in light of recent research as it applies to the topic of spirituality.

[3] Heidelberg Disputation (1518), LW 31:35-70, art. 26-28.

[4] See Heidelberg Disputation (1518), On Two Kinds of Righteousness (1519), On the Freedom of a Christian (1520), LW 31:293-306, 31:327-382. Also, Luther's Confession Concerning Christ's Supper (1528), LW 37:151-372; Large Catechism (1529), in *The Book of Concord*, ed. Wengert and Kolb, 2000.

[5] For important studies of the Reformation's impact on women's lives, see Roper 1989; Marshall 1989; Wiesner 1999, Treu 1999.

[6] Some of the most visible changes with the Reformation were the distribution of Communion in both kinds, changing the practice of repentance (from four parts to two parts), and allowing clergy marriage. Also, abolishing certain traditions such as the various cults of saints and religious festivals very concretely changed people's spiritual lives.

[7] Note has been removed

[8] N.b. The fact that the Finnish language does not distinguish masculine and feminine gender in the third person personal pronoun is not reflected in the English translation.

[9] In other words, "Vergöttlichung" is understood by Luther as the union of Logos and flesh, word and human. As an important point of clarification, Mannermaa reminds that this does not mean any change in either substance, as each retains its own properties; the union can be seen as community of being (Mannermaa 1998, 6).

[10] See the explanation of the Creed, third part, in Small and Large Catechism.

[11] "This is the main idea of Catechism: through faith and meditation a Christian receives the spiritual gifts in Christ and participates in God" (Peura 2000, 23-24).

[12] See Hendrix 1999, 256, 258-259. Also Peura 2000, 17. According to Peura, in catechetic living of the Word, we become partakers of God and transformed into God. "We can, therefore, speak about salvation as a *participation in* God or as *theosis* in a genuine Lutheran sense of the word" (Peura 2000, 29)

[13] In his post-humously published *Theology of the Heart: The Role of Mysticism in the Theology of Martin Luther* (1998), Hoffman responds to the critics of his earlier work on Luther and mysticism. To the criticism that he did not "take into consideration 'the epistemological problem,'" Hoffman reiterates that it is precisely the epistemological problem in Luther research that has been his main interest (This has also been of interest to the Finnish Luther scholars).

[14] See Hendrix's evaluation of Hoffman's thesis on mystical theology being about experience of God and spirituality being about "awareness of the presence of the Holy Spirit mediated by the risen Christ" (Hendrix 1999, 261, note 39, 260, note 34).

[15] Hoffmann criticizes Ebeling and others who saw Luther's mysticism as "Augenblicksanliegen," a passing concern that evaporated as he matured (Hoffman 1976, 322). According to Hoffman, Luther spoke the "language of mystical theology" until the end. For Luther, the question of God is a question of experience (ibid., 323). See also 324, 325, 327 for further arguments.

[16] The term mysticism comes with baggage, as Alistair McGrath says; also Hendrix 1999, 260, note 34. Hoffman's Introduction in his 1998 *Theology of the Heart* is an excellent introduction to the perspective to approach Luther's theology as mystical theology; see 1998, 13-28. In addition, see McGinn 1996.

Lament's Hope

[17] Exactly what kind of hope is the question. See the final section of the paper.

[18] NJPS translation. An alternative translation of the final verse, suggested by *The Jewish Study Bible*: "But I trust in your faithfulness, may my heart exult in Your deliverance. May I sing to the LORD because He has been good to me."

[19] This is clearly not true for African American churches.

[20] Luther's first published work dealing with Hebrew was on the penitential psalms. See M. Reu 1934, 116.

[21] I have taught the book of Job on several occasions. In every instance, Lutheran students (whether seminarians or parishioners) have had a difficult time accepting that Job is innocent.

[22] The relationship between lament/complaint and accusation is more obvious in German: "Klage" and "Anklage."

[23] I have revised the translation. See Westermann 1990, 87.

Past Imperfect: Spiritual Lessons from Things Left Behind

[24] Malanchthon Lutheran Church memories, Icelandic Synod newsletter, March, 1962.

Field Education: Rich Soil for Seminarians' Spiritual Formation

[25] Gnosticism is "thought and practice especially of various cults of late pre-Christian and early Christian centuries distinguished by the conviction that matter is evil and that emancipation comes through gnosis [knowledge]." *Ninth New Collegiate Dictionary*, Springfield, MA: Merriam-Webster Inc., 1983.

[26] Brother Lawrence of the Resurrection (Nicholas Herman, c. 1605-1691), a Carmelite lay brother, was a pious man with a contagious faith in an irreligious age among suspicious people. He led an active life that included serving several years as a soldier. Web Site: "Lawrence, Brother (Nicholas Herman, c. 1605-1691)," Christian Classics Ethereal Library at Calvin College, http://www.ccel.org/l/lawrence/.

Teaching Spirituality with Luther and Medieval Women Mystics

[27] Many of the medieval women mystics have been already introduced in the foundational series, *The Classics of Western Spirituality*, Paulist Press.

[28] I have discussed the meaning, relevance, and challenges of medieval women for contemporary people and proposed constructive ways to assess their legacy. See Stjerna 2001; Stjerna 2002.

[29] Caroline Walker Bynum has pioneered in examining the gender aspect and its irrelevance as well as relevance in women's religious life in the Middle Ages. See Bynum 1991.

[30] For a summa of Luther's spiritual teaching, one can consult Luther's Small and Large Catechism from 1529, included in the new edition of *The Book of Concord*.

[31] See the chapter "Luther-an Spirituality" in this book. Also, Hoffman 1998 for an excellent reflection on Luther's experiential theology.

[32] Most beautifully in my view Luther expresses this theology in his Heidelberg Disputation (1518) and The Freedom of a Christian (1520). See LW 31:39-58, LW 31:333-377.

[33] On this, see On Two Kinds of Righteousness (1519) in LW 31:297-306.

[34] On Luther's view of the sacraments, see e.g., The Babylonian Captivity of the Church (1520), LW 36:11-57; Confession Concerning Christ's Supper, LW 37:206-235, 360-372, and Smalcald Articles (1537), *Book of Concord*, 2000.